STOCK VALUATION HANDBOOK PART 1

Billion Dollar Valuation

BDV Publications

Copyright © 2020 Billion Dollar Valuation

All rights reserved

The characters and events portrayed in this book are fictitious. Any similarity to real persons, living or dead, is coincidental and not intended by the author.

No part of this book may be reproduced, or stored in a retrieval system, or transmitted in any form or by any means, electronic, mechanical, photocopying, recording, or otherwise, without express written permission of the publisher.

Cover design by: BDV Publications
Printed in India

STOCK VALUATION HANDBOOK   PART 1

This is the first DIY Handbook on Discounted Cash flow Valuation of the listed companies in India. Use the values and calculations mentions in this book once you have the excel model downloaded from the link given below.

https://www.eloquens.com/tool/93b3CR0R/billion-dollar-valuation/do-it-yourself-dcf-valuation-blank-template-with-forecasting

The process of valuation is both art and science and hence we leave it up to you for making appropriate assumptions and Formulas. The entire Do-it-yourself valuation takes about 10-15 hours for one company and you can master the process by using this Handbook and our Excel template.

Thorough research is done by our research analysts over a 10 year period on both the qualitative and quantitative factors of these companies. This analysis is then used to forecast financial statements over a period of 5 years.

Hundreds of Annual reports, Investor presentations, Management commentary and Con-call transcripts have been analysed to gather data and analyse the business model and financial conditions. The books do not have any relation with one another and analyses a completely different set of companies each. You can start with any random book from the series and need not begin with the first book.

(Note: All the research done by us is only for educational purposes and should not be seen as Investment recommendations. We are Research analyst and not a SEBI registered Investment Advisor. Our research completely reflects our personal opinions and not of any of our current or previous employers. Kindly do your own due diligence before Investing)

INDRAPRASTHA GAS VALUATION

Indraprastha Gas Valuation

Indraprastha Gas Valuation: About the Company

Incorporated in 1998, IGL took over Delhi City Gas Distribution Project in 1999 from GAIL (India) Limited (Formerly Gas Authority of India Limited). With the backing of strong promoters – GAIL (India) Ltd. and Bharat Petroleum Corporation Ltd. (BPCL) – IGL plans to provide natural gas in the entire capital region. The company operates in the Utility industry where market dominance comes through scale, distribution network, licensing and capacity. IGL was started to lay the network for the distribution of natural gas in Delhi to consumers in the domestic, transport, and commercial sectors. Today IGL has its operations in NCT of Delhi, Noida, Greater Noida, Ghaziabad, Rewari, Karnal and Muzaffarnagar with 555+ CNG stations, 13.75+ lacs residential consumers and 5600+ industrial / commercial customers. From here, we go ahead with Indraprastha Gas Valuation and Intrinsic Value of its shares.

Read more here: **Indraprastha Gas Shares Fundamental Analysis**

Methodology Used:

Discounted cash flow (DCF) is a valuation method used to estimate the value of an investment based on its expected future cash flows. DCF analysis attempts to figure out the value of an investment today, based on projections of how much money it will generate in the future. The following step by step procedure is followed.

1. Determining the Revenue Growth Rates
2. Forecasting the Financial Statements
3. Deriving the FCFF and FCFE
4. Calculating the Terminal Value
5. Calculating the Discount Rate
6. Discounting the Cashflows
7. Arriving at the Intrinsic Value of the Shares

Step 1: Determining the Revenue Growth Rates

We arrive at the below table by using the past and expected future performance of both the company and the economy. This along with adjustments to changes in the management expect-

ations, extraordinary events and other macro factors give the revenue growth rates for Indraprastha Gas Valuation.

Financial Year	Revenue Growth Rate
Year 1	12%
Year 2	-20%
Year 3	35%
Year 4	18%
Year 5	15%

Revenue Growth Rates: Indraprastha Gas Valuation

Step 2: Forecasting the Financial Statements

The financial statements are forecasted for a period of 5 years using the annual report data of the company. The assumptions used for forecasting are tabulated below. The Excel model is completely editable and can be adjusted for specific changes which may happen over a period of time.

BILLION DOLLAR VALUATION

Assumptions Control Sheet	
Income Statement	
Average COGS as Percentage of Revenue	70.72%
Research and Development as Percentage of Revenue	0.00%
Sales, General and administrative as Percentage of Revenue	0.75%
Other operating expenses as Percentage of Revenue	9.58%
Other income (expense) as Percentage of Revenue	2.65%
Balance Sheet	
Short Term Debt as Percentage of Total Assets	0.00%
Long Term Debt as Percentage of Total Assets	3.30%
Cash and Cash Equivalents as Percentage of Revenue	5.05%
Short Term Equivalents as Percentage of Revenue	23.25%
Accounts Receivables as Percentage of Revenue	5.33%
Inventory as Percentage of Revenue	1.23%
Prepaid Expenses as Percentage of Revenue	0.42%
Other Current Assets as Percentage of Revenue	0.98%
Gross property, plant and equipment as Percentage of Revenue	67.57%
Intangible assets as Percentage of Revenue	0.34%
Other long-term assets as Percentage of Revenue	9.88%
Accounts payable as Percentage of Revenue	6.61%
Corporate Tax Rate	22.00%
Other current liabilities as Percentage of Revenue	16.42%
Retained Earnings as as Percentage of Net Income	79.49%
Accumulated other comprehensive income as Percentage of Revenue	6.86%
Cashflow Statement	
Other Working Capital as Percentage of Revenue	-3.25%

Financial Statements Forecast :Indraprastha Gas Valuation

Step 3: Deriving the FCFF and FCFE

Free cash flow to the firm (FCFF) represents the amount of cash flow from operations available for distribution after accounting for depreciation expenses, taxes, working capital, and investments. FCFF is a measurement of a company's profitability after all expenses and reinvestments. It is given as follows.

Free cash flow to equity (FCFE) is a measure of how much cash is available to the equity shareholders of a company after all expenses, reinvestment, and debt are paid. FCFE is a measure of equity capital usage.

F/S Items (INR Millions)	Mar-20	Mar-21	Mar-22	Mar-23	Mar-24

Free Cash Flow to Firm	10330	7266	10855	13013	15858
Free Cash Flow to Equity	12613	7182	11128	13267	16139

FCFF and FCFE values: Indraprastha Gas Valuation

Step 4: Calculating the Terminal Value

Terminal value (TV) is the value of a business or project beyond the forecast period when future cash flows can be estimated. It assumes that a business will grow at a set growth rate forever after the forecast period. Terminal value often comprises a large percentage of the total assessed value.

Terminal Value Calculation	Units INR Millions
Free Cash Flow to Firm	15858.11
Growth Rate	5.00%
Cost of Capital	11.99%
Terminal Value	238127.47

Terminal Value: Indraprastha Gas Valuation

Step 5: Calculating the Discount Rate

DCF analysis helps assess the viability of a project or investment by calculating the present value of expected future cash flows using a discount rate. Here we use the Weighted average cost of capital (WACC) to discount the cash flow. The below table from the excel model shows the calculation of WACC for Indraprastha Gas Valuation.

Cost of Equity Calcuation using CAPM	
Risk Free Rate (5 year G-Sec)	5.18%
Stock Beta (Ref: Reuters)	0.74
Beta Unlevered B/(1+ D(1-t)/E)	0.74
Beta Relevered B*(1+ D(1-t)/E)	0.77
Market Return Rm (Nifty 50 10 Year CAGR)	14.25%
Cost of Equity	**12.13%**

Cost of Debt	
Cost of Debt (Interest Expense/Total Debt)	**9.00%**

Cost of Capital	
Cost of Equity	12.13%
Weight of Equity in Target Capital Structure	95.70%
Cost of Debt	9.00%
Weight of Debt in Capital Structure	4.30%
WACC	**11.99%**

WACC Calculation for Indraprastha Gas Valuation.

Step 6: Discounting the Cashflows

The WACC and the Cost of Equity for the company calculated in the above step are then used to discount the FCFF, FCFE and Terminal Value calculated in Step 3 and 4. In our case, we'll only consider the FCFF based Intrinsic price of the shares as it represents the cash flow to all the suppliers of capital and not only to the equity shareholders. Thus we arrive at Present value of future FCFF for Indraprastha Gas Valuation. (Units are INR Millions)

FCFF Calculation	FV	Discounted
Mar-20	10330.25	9224.05
Mar-21	7265.99	5793.18
Mar-22	10855.16	7728.05
Mar-23	13013.03	8272.24
Mar-24	15858.11	9001.34
Terminal Value	238127.47	135165.29
Present Value (PV)		175184.15

FCFE Calculation	FV	Discounted
Mar-20	12612.68	11248.58
Mar-21	7182.37	5712.80
Mar-22	11128.10	7893.91
Mar-23	13266.78	8393.20
Mar-24	16138.89	9105.97
Terminal Value	238127.47	134357.53
Present Value (PV)		176711.99

PV of FCFF and FCFE for Indraprastha Gas Valuation.

Step 7: Arriving at the Intrinsic Value of the Shares

Dividing the PV of the FCFF and Terminal Value (the Value of the entire firm) by the number of outstanding shares we get the per share intrinsic value. We can compare this price with the current market price of the stock to get the Discount or Premium to its intrinsic price.

Indraprastha Gas Valuation	Units
PV in INR Million	175184
No of Shares Outstanding (In Million)	700

Intrinsic Value	250.26
Current Market Price of Share	444.00
Current Discount/Premium	77%

Intrinsic Value of the Shares: Indraprastha Gas Valuation

Indraprastha Gas Valuation and Intrinsic Share Price = INR 250.26

HINDALCO VALUATION

DCF Valuation

Hindalco Valuation: About the Company

Hindalco is the flagship company of the Aditya Birla Group. The company operates in three business segments namely primary aluminium, downstream aluminium and copper. One of their subsidiaries called Novelis in North America is the world's largest aluminium Flat Rolled Products (FRP) producer and recycler. Hindalco's domestic aluminium plants have a production capacity of 1.3 million tonnes per annum. They are present across the manufacturing value chain from bauxite, mining, alumina refining, smelting to downstream rolling, extrusions and foils. From here, we go ahead with Hindalco Valuation and Intrinsic Value of its shares.

Read more here: **Hindalco Shares Fundamental Analysis**

Methodology Used:

Discounted cash flow (DCF) is a valuation method used to estimate the value of an investment based on its expected future cash flows. DCF analysis attempts to figure out the value of an investment today, based on projections of how much money it will generate in the future. The following step by step procedure is followed.

1. Determining the Revenue Growth Rates
2. Forecasting the Financial Statements
3. Deriving the FCFF and FCFE
4. Calculating the Terminal Value
5. Calculating the Discount Rate
6. Discounting the Cashflows
7. Arriving at the Intrinsic Value of the Shares

Step 1: Determining the Revenue Growth Rates

We arrive at the below table by using the past and expected future performance of both the company and the economy. This along with adjustments to changes in the management expectations, extraordinary events and other macro factors give the revenue growth rates for Hindalco Valuation.

Financial Year	Revenue Growth Rate
Year 1	-9%
Year 2	6%
Year 3	13%
Year 4	9%
Year 5	5%

Revenue Growth Rates: Hindalco Valuation

Step 2: Forecasting the Financial Statements

The financial statements are forecasted for a period of 5 years using the annual report data of the company. The assumptions used for forecasting are tabulated below. The Excel model is completely editable and can be adjusted for specific changes which may happen over a period of time.

Assumptions Control Sheet	
Income Statement	
Average COGS as Percentage of Revenue	66.11%
Research and Development as Percentage of Revenue	0.38%
Sales, General and administrative as Percentage of Revenue	0.23%
Other operating expenses as Percentage of Revenue	26.34%
Other income (expense) as Percentage of Revenue	0.49%
Balance Sheet	
Short Term Debt as Percentage of Total Assets	6.09%
Long Term Debt as Percentage of Total Assets	33.40%
Cash and Cash Equivalents as Percentage of Revenue	6.25%
Short Term Equivalents as Percentage of Revenue	5.92%
Accounts Receivables as Percentage of Revenue	8.54%
Inventory as Percentage of Revenue	17.96%
Prepaid Expenses as Percentage of Revenue	1.83%
Other Current Assets as Percentage of Revenue	4.54%
Gross property, plant and equipment as Percentage of Revenue	91.56%
Intangible assets as Percentage of Revenue	3.50%
Other long-term assets as Percentage of Revenue	7.42%
Accounts payable as Percentage of Revenue	16.36%
Corporate Tax Rate	22.00%
Other current liabilities as Percentage of Revenue	6.28%
Retained Earnings as as Percentage of Net Income	89.36%
Accumulated other comprehensive income as Percentage of Revenue	29.93%
Cashflow Statement	
Other Working Capital as Percentage of Revenue	0.00%

Financial Statements Forecast : Hindalco Valuation

Step 3: Deriving the FCFF and FCFE

Free cash flow to the firm (FCFF) represents the amount of cash flow from operations available for distribution after accounting for depreciation expenses, taxes, working capital, and investments. FCFF is a measurement of a company's profitability after all expenses and reinvestments. It is given as follows.

Free cash flow to equity (FCFE) is a measure of how much cash is available to the equity shareholders of a company after all expenses, reinvestment, and debt are paid. FCFE is a measure of equity capital usage.

F/S Items (INR Millions)	Mar-20	Mar-21	Mar-22	Mar-23	Mar-24

| Free Cash Flow to Firm | 94006 | 50037 | -34821 | 7383 | 60594 |
| Free Cash Flow to Equity | 309002 | -17723 | -92540 | 7658 | 51996 |

FCFF and FCFE values: Hindalco Valuation

Step 4: Calculating the Terminal Value

Terminal value (TV) is the value of a business or project beyond the forecast period when future cash flows can be estimated. It assumes that a business will grow at a set growth rate forever after the forecast period. Terminal value often comprises a large percentage of the total assessed value.

Terminal Value Calculation	Units INR Millions
Free Cash Flow to Firm	60593.94
Growth Rate	5.00%
Cost of Capital	13.82%
Terminal Value	721722.79

Terminal Value: Hindalco Valuation

Step 5: Calculating the Discount Rate

DCF analysis helps assess the viability of a project or investment by calculating the present value of expected future cash flows using a discount rate. Here we use the Weighted average cost of capital (WACC) to discount the cash flow. The below table from the excel model shows the calculation of WACC for Hindalco Valuation.

Cost of Equity Calcuation using CAPM	
Risk Free Rate (5 year G-Sec)	5.18%
Stock Beta (Ref: Reuters)	1.51
Beta Unlevered B/(1+ D(1-t)/E)	0.88
Beta Relevered B*(1+ D(1-t)/E)	1.73
Market Return Rm (Nifty 50 10 Year CAGR)	14.25%
Cost of Equity	**20.88%**

Cost of Debt	
Cost of Debt (Interest Expense/Total Debt)	8.08%

Cost of Capital	
Cost of Equity	20.88%
Weight of Equity in Target Capital Structure	44.82%
Cost of Debt	8.08%
Weight of Debt in Capital Structure	55.18%
WACC	**13.82%**

WACC Calculation for Hindalco Valuation.

Step 6: Discounting the Cashflows

The WACC and the Cost of Equity for the company calculated in the above step are then used to discount the FCFF, FCFE and Terminal Value calculated in Step 3 and 4. In our case, we'll only consider the FCFF based Intrinsic price of the shares as it represents the cash flow to all the suppliers of capital and not only to the equity shareholders. Thus we arrive at Present value of future FCFF for Hindalco Valuation. (Units are INR Millions)

FCFF Calculation	FV	Discounted
Mar-20	94006.08	82595.13
Mar-21	50036.62	38626.46
Mar-22	-34821.25	-23617.83
Mar-23	7382.93	4399.69
Mar-24	60593.94	31726.47
Terminal Value	721722.79	377887.84
Present Value (PV)		511617.77

FCFE Calculation	FV	Discounted
Mar-20	309002.30	255623.21
Mar-21	-17722.69	-12128.49
Mar-22	-92540.08	-52389.66
Mar-23	7657.89	3586.44
Mar-24	51995.82	20144.72
Terminal Value	721722.79	279616.80
Present Value (PV)		494453.01

PV of FCFF and FCFE for Hindalco Valuation.

Step 7: Arriving at the Intrinsic Value of the Shares

Dividing the PV of the FCFF and Terminal Value (the Value of the entire firm) by the number of outstanding shares we get the per share intrinsic value. We can compare this price with the current market price of the stock to get the Discount or Premium to its intrinsic price.

Hindalco Valuation	Units
PV in INR Million	511618
No of Shares Outstanding (In Million)	2228

Intrinsic Value	229.63
Current Market Price of Share	221.85
Current Discount/Premium	-3%

Intrinsic Value of the Shares: Hindalco Valuation

Hindalco Valuation and Intrinsic Share Price = INR 229.63

GSK PHARMA VALUATION

GSK Pharma Valuation : About the Company

STOCK VALUATION HANDBOOK PART 1

GSK Pharmaceuticals Ltd is an Indian subsidiary of GlaxoSmithKline PLC which is one of the world's leading research-based pharmaceutical and healthcare companies. It is one of the oldest pharmaceuticals companies in India and manufactures prescription medicines and vaccines. They are focused on science related to the immune system, use of genetics and advanced technologies. From here, we go ahead with GSK Pharma Valuation and Intrinsic Value of its shares.

Read more here: GSK Pharma Shares Fundamental Analysis

Methodology Used:

Discounted cash flow (DCF) is a valuation method used to estimate the value of an investment based on its expected future cash flows. DCF analysis attempts to figure out the value of an investment today, based on projections of how much money it will generate in the future. The following step by step procedure is followed.

1. Determining the Revenue Growth Rates
2. Forecasting the Financial Statements
3. Deriving the FCFF and FCFE
4. Calculating the Terminal Value
5. Calculating the Discount Rate
6. Discounting the Cashflows
7. Arriving at the Intrinsic Value of the Shares

Step 1: Determining the Revenue Growth Rates

We arrive at the below table by using the past and expected future performance of both the company and the economy. This along with adjustments to changes in the management expect-

ations, extraordinary events and other macro factors give the revenue growth rates for GSK Pharma Valuation.

Financial Year	Revenue Growth Rate
Year 1	3%
Year 2	5%
Year 3	12%
Year 4	10%
Year 5	11%

Revenue Growth Rates: GSK Pharma Valuation

Step 2: Forecasting the Financial Statements

The financial statements are forecasted for a period of 5 years using the annual report data of the company. The assumptions used for forecasting are tabulated below. The Excel model is completely editable and can be adjusted for specific changes which may happen over a period of time.

Assumptions Control Sheet	
Income Statement	
Average COGS as Percentage of Revenue	48.87%
Research and Development as Percentage of Revenue	0.00%
Sales, General and administrative as Percentage of Revenue	10.53%
Other operating expenses as Percentage of Revenue	23.44%
Other income (expense) as Percentage of Revenue	4.19%
Balance Sheet	
Short Term Debt as Percentage of Total Assets	0.02%
Long Term Debt as Percentage of Total Assets	0.04%
Cash and Cash Equivalents as Percentage of Revenue	9.89%
Short Term Equivalents as Percentage of Revenue	#DIV/0!
Accounts Receivables as Percentage of Revenue	4.68%
Inventory as Percentage of Revenue	16.29%
Prepaid Expenses as Percentage of Revenue	1.62%
Other Current Assets as Percentage of Revenue	42.14%
Gross property, plant and equipment as Percentage of Revenue	30.53%
Intangible assets as Percentage of Revenue	2.00%
Other long-term assets as Percentage of Revenue	12.94%
Accounts payable as Percentage of Revenue	16.82%
Corporate Tax Rate	22.00%
Other current liabilities as Percentage of Revenue	14.98%
Retained Earnings as as Percentage of Net Income	18.52%
Accumulated other comprehensive income as Percentage of Revenue	29.84%
Cashflow Statement	
Other Working Capital as Percentage of Revenue	-1.36%

Financial Statements Forecast : GSK Pharma Valuation

Step 3: Deriving the FCFF and FCFE

Free cash flow to the firm (FCFF) represents the amount of cash flow from operations available for distribution after accounting for depreciation expenses, taxes, working capital, and investments. FCFF is a measurement of a company's profitability after all expenses and reinvestments. It is given as follows.

Free cash flow to equity (FCFE) is a measure of how much cash is available to the equity shareholders of a company after all expenses, reinvestment, and debt are paid. FCFE is a measure of equity capital usage.

F/S Items (INR Millions)	Mar-20	Mar-21	Mar-22	Mar-23	Mar-24

Free Cash Flow to Firm	2653	4135	3380	4314	4729
Free Cash Flow to Equity	2666	4135	3381	4314	4730

FCFF and FCFE values: GSK Pharma Valuation

Step 4: Calculating the Terminal Value

Terminal value (TV) is the value of a business or project beyond the forecast period when future cash flows can be estimated. It assumes that a business will grow at a set growth rate forever after the forecast period. Terminal value often comprises a large percentage of the total assessed value.

Terminal Value Calculation	Units INR Millions
Free Cash Flow to Firm	4728.75
Growth Rate	5.00%
Cost of Capital	6.72%
Terminal Value	288132.18

Terminal Value: GSK Pharma Valuation

Step 5: Calculating the Discount Rate

DCF analysis helps assess the viability of a project or investment by calculating the present value of expected future cash flows using a discount rate. Here we use the Weighted average cost of capital (WACC) to discount the cash flow. The below table from the excel model shows the calculation of WACC for GSK Pharma Valuation.

Cost of Equity Calcuation using CAPM	
Risk Free Rate (5 year G-Sec)	5.18%
Stock Beta (Ref: Reuters)	0.17
Beta Unlevered B/(1+ D(1-t)/E)	0.17
Beta Relevered B*(1+ D(1-t)/E)	0.17
Market Return Rm (Nifty 50 10 Year CAGR)	14.25%
Cost of Equity	**6.72%**

Cost of Debt	
Cost of Debt (Interest Expense/Total Debt)	7.14%

Cost of Capital	
Cost of Equity	6.72%
Weight of Equity in Target Capital Structure	99.90%
Cost of Debt	7.14%
Weight of Debt in Capital Structure	0.10%
WACC	**6.72%**

WACC Calculation for GSK Pharma Valuation.

Step 6: Discounting the Cashflows

The WACC and the Cost of Equity for the company calculated in the above step are then used to discount the FCFF, FCFE and Terminal Value calculated in Step 3 and 4. In our case, we'll only consider the FCFF based Intrinsic price of the shares as it represents the cash flow to all the suppliers of capital and not only to the equity shareholders. Thus we arrive at Present value of future FCFF for GSK Pharma Valuation. (Units are INR Millions)

FCFF Calculation	FV	Discounted
Mar-20	2653.36	2486.20
Mar-21	4135.41	3630.78
Mar-22	3380.31	2780.86
Mar-23	4313.56	3325.07
Mar-24	4728.75	3415.48
Terminal Value	288132.18	208111.90
Present Value (PV)		223750.29

FCFE Calculation	FV	Discounted
Mar-20	2665.83	2497.90
Mar-21	4135.23	3630.65
Mar-22	3381.46	2781.84
Mar-23	4314.42	3325.78
Mar-24	4729.93	3416.40
Terminal Value	288132.18	208116.07
Present Value (PV)		223768.65

PV of FCFF and FCFE for GSK Pharma Valuation.

Step 7: Arriving at the Intrinsic Value of the Shares

Dividing the PV of the FCFF and Terminal Value (the Value of the entire firm) by the number of outstanding shares we get the per share intrinsic value. We can compare this price with the current market price of the stock to get the Discount or Premium to its intrinsic price.

GSK Pharma Valuation	Units
PV in INR Million	223750
No of Shares Outstanding (In Million)	169

Intrinsic Value	1323.97
Current Market Price of Share	1466.00
Current Discount/Premium	11%

Intrinsic Value of the Shares: GSK Pharma Valuation

GSK Pharma Valuation and Intrinsic Share Price = INR 1323.97

GAIL VALUATION

GAIL (INDIA) Ltd.
Valuation

GAIL Valuation: About the Company

GAIL (India) Ltd was incorporated in 1984 as a Central Public Sector Undertaking (PSU) under the Ministry of Petroleum & Natural Gas. The company was initially given the responsibility of construction, operation & maintenance of the HVJ pipeline Project. Today, Gail is the largest state-owned natural gas processing and distribution company in India. From here, we go ahead with GAIL Valuation and Intrinsic Value of its shares.

Read more here: **GAIL Shares Fundamental Analysis**

Methodology Used:

Discounted cash flow (DCF) is a valuation method used to estimate the value of an investment based on its expected future cash flows. DCF analysis attempts to figure out the value of an investment today, based on projections of how much money it will generate in the future. The following step by step procedure is followed.

1. Determining the Revenue Growth Rates
2. Forecasting the Financial Statements
3. Deriving the FCFF and FCFE
4. Calculating the Terminal Value
5. Calculating the Discount Rate
6. Discounting the Cashflows
7. Arriving at the Intrinsic Value of the Shares

Step 1: Determining the Revenue Growth Rates

We arrive at the below table by using the past and expected future performance of both the company and the economy. This along with adjustments to changes in the management expect-

ations, extraordinary events and other macro factors give the revenue growth rates for GAIL Valuation.

Financial Year	Revenue Growth Rate
Year 1	-40%
Year 2	-20%
Year 3	50%
Year 4	28%
Year 5	20%

Revenue Growth Rates: GAIL Valuation

Step 2: Forecasting the Financial Statements

The financial statements are forecasted for a period of 5 years using the annual report data of the company. The assumptions used for forecasting are tabulated below. The Excel model is completely editable and can be adjusted for specific changes which may happen over a period of time.

Assumptions Control Sheet	
Income Statement	
Average COGS as Percentage of Revenue	83.29%
Research and Development as Percentage of Revenue	0.05%
Sales, General and administrative as Percentage of Revenue	0.40%
Other operating expenses as Percentage of Revenue	6.65%
Other income (expense) as Percentage of Revenue	1.61%
Balance Sheet	
Short Term Debt as Percentage of Total Assets	3.31%
Long Term Debt as Percentage of Total Assets	6.18%
Cash and Cash Equivalents as Percentage of Revenue	1.80%
Short Term Equivalents as Percentage of Revenue	0.65%
Accounts Receivables as Percentage of Revenue	5.63%
Inventory as Percentage of Revenue	3.33%
Prepaid Expenses as Percentage of Revenue	1.12%
Other Current Assets as Percentage of Revenue	5.35%
Gross property, plant and equipment as Percentage of Revenue	65.24%
Intangible assets as Percentage of Revenue	1.92%
Other long-term assets as Percentage of Revenue	26.61%
Accounts payable as Percentage of Revenue	5.79%
Corporate Tax Rate	22.00%
Other current liabilities as Percentage of Revenue	8.17%
Retained Earnings as as Percentage of Net Income	59.14%
Accumulated other comprehensive income as Percentage of Revenue	34.42%
Cashflow Statement	
Other Working Capital as Percentage of Revenue	-0.07%

Financial Statements Forecast : GAIL Valuation

Step 3: Deriving the FCFF and FCFE

Free cash flow to the firm (FCFF) represents the amount of cash flow from operations available for distribution after accounting for depreciation expenses, taxes, working capital, and investments. FCFF is a measurement of a company's profitability after all expenses and reinvestments. It is given as follows.

Free cash flow to equity (FCFE) is a measure of how much cash is available to the equity shareholders of a company after all expenses, reinvestment, and debt are paid. FCFE is a measure of equity capital usage.

F/S Items (INR Millions)	Mar-20	Mar-21	Mar-22	Mar-23	Mar-24

Free Cash Flow to Firm	20001	6479	63632	63569	68256
Free Cash Flow to Equity	47537	2581	65322	65505	70410

FCFF and FCFE values: GAIL Valuation

Step 4: Calculating the Terminal Value

Terminal value (TV) is the value of a business or project beyond the forecast period when future cash flows can be estimated. It assumes that a business will grow at a set growth rate forever after the forecast period. Terminal value often comprises a large percentage of the total assessed value.

Terminal Value Calculation	Units INR Millions
Free Cash Flow to Firm	68255.95
Growth Rate	5.00%
Cost of Capital	11.06%
Terminal Value	1182304.80

Terminal Value: GAIL Valuation

Step 5: Calculating the Discount Rate

DCF analysis helps assess the viability of a project or investment by calculating the present value of expected future cash flows using a discount rate. Here we use the Weighted average cost of capital (WACC) to discount the cash flow. The below table from the excel model shows the calculation of WACC for GAIL Valuation.

Cost of Equity Calcuation using CAPM	
Risk Free Rate (5 year G-Sec)	5.18%
Stock Beta (Ref: Reuters)	0.68
Beta Unlevered B/(1+ D(1-t)/E)	0.64
Beta Relevered B*(1+ D(1-t)/E)	0.72
Market Return Rm (Nifty 50 10 Year CAGR)	14.25%
Cost of Equity	**11.67%**

Cost of Debt	
Cost of Debt (Interest Expense/Total Debt)	**6.91%**

Cost of Capital	
Cost of Equity	11.67%
Weight of Equity in Target Capital Structure	87.31%
Cost of Debt	6.91%
Weight of Debt in Capital Structure	12.69%
WACC	**11.06%**

WACC Calculation for GAIL Valuation.

Step 6: Discounting the Cashflows

The WACC and the Cost of Equity for the company calculated in the above step are then used to discount the FCFF, FCFE and Terminal Value calculated in Step 3 and 4. In our case, we'll only consider the FCFF based Intrinsic price of the shares as it represents the cash flow to all the suppliers of capital and not only to the equity shareholders. Thus we arrive at Present value of future FCFF for GAIL Valuation. (Units are INR Millions)

FCFF Calculation	FV	Discounted
Mar-20	20000.84	18008.75
Mar-21	6479.32	5252.91
Mar-22	63631.98	46449.55
Mar-23	63568.84	41781.66
Mar-24	68255.95	40394.04
Terminal Value	1182304.80	699690.93
Present Value (PV)		851577.85

FCFE Calculation	FV	Discounted
Mar-20	47536.78	42570.58
Mar-21	2581.41	2070.22
Mar-22	65322.45	46913.94
Mar-23	65504.71	42130.03
Mar-24	70410.38	40554.19
Terminal Value	1182304.80	680970.88
Present Value (PV)		855209.85

PV of FCFF and FCFE for GAIL Valuation.

Step 7: Arriving at the Intrinsic Value of the Shares

Dividing the PV of the FCFF and Terminal Value (the Value of the entire firm) by the number of outstanding shares we get the per share intrinsic value. We can compare this price with the current market price of the stock to get the Discount or Premium to its intrinsic price.

GAIL Valuation	Units
PV in INR Million	851578
No of Shares Outstanding (In Million)	4510

Intrinsic Value	188.82
Current Market Price of Share	93.65
Current Discount/Premium	-50%

Intrinsic Value of the Shares: GAIL Valuation

GAIL Valuation and Intrinsic Share Price = INR 188.82

ABB INDIA VALUATION

ABB India Valuation : About the Company

ABB India has a resilient and diversified business model which helps them to drive growth. Since the last few years, it has shown revenue growth across emerging segments and a solid cash position. It has around 70+ years of presence in India and is promoted by the Swiss giant ABB Schweiz AG. The company competes with some other big names in electrification and automation like FESTO, Crompton Greaves and Honeywell all of which are foreign-based. They are all competing for the emerging market in India with their foreign technology. Since the Industry is asset-heavy entry of new players is difficult. From here, we go ahead with ABB India Valuation and Intrinsic Value of its shares.

Read more here: **ABB India Shares Fundamental Analysis**

Methodology Used:

Discounted cash flow (DCF) is a valuation method used to estimate the value of an investment based on its expected future cash flows. DCF analysis attempts to figure out the value of an investment today, based on projections of how much money it will generate in the future. The following step by step procedure is followed.

1. Determining the Revenue Growth Rates
2. Forecasting the Financial Statements
3. Deriving the FCFF and FCFE
4. Calculating the Terminal Value
5. Calculating the Discount Rate
6. Discounting the Cashflows
7. Arriving at the Intrinsic Value of the Shares

Step 1: Determining the Revenue Growth Rates

We arrive at the below table by using the past and expected future performance of both the company and the economy. This along with adjustments to changes in the management expectations, extraordinary events and other macro factors give the revenue growth rates for ABB India Valuation.

Financial Year	Revenue Growth Rate
Year 1	-20%
Year 2	23%
Year 3	12%
Year 4	10%
Year 5	11%

Revenue Growth Rates: ABB India Valuation

Step 2: Forecasting the Financial Statements

The financial statements are forecasted for a period of 5 years using the annual report data of the company. The assumptions used for forecasting are tabulated below. The Excel model is completely editable and can be adjusted for specific changes which may happen over a period of time.

Assumptions Control Sheet	
Income Statement	
Average COGS as Percentage of Revenue	65.00%
Research and Development as Percentage of Revenue	0.00%
Sales, General and administrative as Percentage of Revenue	2.00%
Other operating expenses as Percentage of Revenue	16.50%
Other income (expense) as Percentage of Revenue	-0.68%
Balance Sheet	
Short Term Debt as Percentage of Total Assets	4.05%
Long Term Debt as Percentage of Total Assets	7.51%
Cash and Cash Equivalents as Percentage of Revenue	13.36%
Short Term Equivalents as Percentage of Revenue	0.73%
Accounts Receivables as Percentage of Revenue	29.69%
Inventory as Percentage of Revenue	13.09%
Prepaid Expenses as Percentage of Revenue	1.13%
Other Current Assets as Percentage of Revenue	25.20%
Gross property, plant and equipment as Percentage of Revenue	19.35%
Intangible assets as Percentage of Revenue	0.52%
Other long-term assets as Percentage of Revenue	6.02%
Accounts payable as Percentage of Revenue	29.06%
Corporate Tax Rate	22.00%
Other current liabilities as Percentage of Revenue	27.07%
Retained Earnings as as Percentage of Net Income	78.37%
Accumulated other comprehensive income as Percentage of Revenue	39.94%
Cashflow Statement	
Other Working Capital as Percentage of Revenue	-1.25%

Financial Statements Forecast : ABB India Valuation

Step 3: Deriving the FCFF and FCFE

Free cash flow to the firm (FCFF) represents the amount of cash flow from operations available for distribution after accounting for depreciation expenses, taxes, working capital, and investments. FCFF is a measurement of a company's profitability after all expenses and reinvestments. It is given as follows.

Free cash flow to equity (FCFE) is a measure of how much cash is available to the equity shareholders of a company after all expenses, reinvestment, and debt are paid. FCFE is a measure of equity capital usage.

F/S Items (INR Millions)	Mar-20	Mar-21	Mar-22	Mar-23	Mar-24

Free Cash Flow to Firm	7304	6251	7959	9064	10366
Free Cash Flow to Equity	16758	7315	8709	9794	11230

FCFF and FCFE values: ABB India Valuation

Step 4: Calculating the Terminal Value

Terminal value (TV) is the value of a business or project beyond the forecast period when future cash flows can be estimated. It assumes that a business will grow at a set growth rate forever after the forecast period. Terminal value often comprises a large percentage of the total assessed value.

Terminal Value Calculation	Units INR Millions
Free Cash Flow to Firm	10365.98
Growth Rate	5.00%
Cost of Capital	14.32%
Terminal Value	116810.40

Terminal Value: ABB India Valuation

Step 5: Calculating the Discount Rate

DCF analysis helps assess the viability of a project or investment by calculating the present value of expected future cash flows using a discount rate. Here we use the Weighted average cost of capital (WACC) to discount the cash flow. The below table from the excel model shows the calculation of WACC for ABB India Valuation.

Cost of Equity Calcuation using CAPM	
Risk Free Rate (5 year G-Sec)	5.18%
Stock Beta (Ref: Reuters)	1.00
Beta Unlevered B/(1+ D(1-t)/E)	1.00
Beta Relevered B*(1+ D(1-t)/E)	1.17
Market Return Rm (Nifty 50 10 Year CAGR)	14.25%
Cost of Equity	**15.83%**

Cost of Debt	
Cost of Debt (Interest Expense/Total Debt)	**7.55%**

Cost of Capital	
Cost of Equity	15.83%
Weight of Equity in Target Capital Structure	81.72%
Cost of Debt	7.55%
Weight of Debt in Capital Structure	18.28%
WACC	**14.32%**

WACC Calculation for ABB India Valuation.

Step 6: Discounting the Cashflows

The WACC and the Cost of Equity for the company calculated in the above step are then used to discount the FCFF, FCFE and Terminal Value calculated in Step 3 and 4. In our case, we'll only consider the FCFF based Intrinsic price of the shares as it represents the cash flow to all the suppliers of capital and not only to the equity shareholders. Thus we arrive at Present value of future FCFF for ABB India Valuation. (Units are INR Millions)

FCFF Calculation	FV	Discounted
Mar-20	7304.34	6389.50
Mar-21	6250.77	4783.05
Mar-22	7958.61	5327.14
Mar-23	9064.05	5307.20
Mar-24	10365.98	5309.32
Terminal Value	116810.40	59828.80
Present Value (PV)		86945.02

FCFE Calculation	FV	Discounted
Mar-20	16758.44	14467.87
Mar-21	7315.14	5452.11
Mar-22	8708.87	5603.70
Mar-23	9793.51	5440.29
Mar-24	11230.14	5385.67
Terminal Value	116810.40	56019.08
Present Value (PV)		92368.70

PV of FCFF and FCFE for ABB India Valuation.

Step 7: Arriving at the Intrinsic Value of the Shares

Dividing the PV of the FCFF and Terminal Value (the Value of the entire firm) by the number of outstanding shares we get the per share intrinsic value. We can compare this price with the current market price of the stock to get the Discount or Premium to its intrinsic price.

ABB India Valuation	Units
PV in INR Million	86945
No of Shares Outstanding (In Million)	212

Intrinsic Value	410.12
Current Market Price of Share	948.00
Current Discount/Premium	131%

Intrinsic Value of the Shares: ABB India Valuation

ABB India Valuation and Intrinsic Share Price = INR 410.12

BLUE STAR VALUATION

STOCK VALUATION HANDBOOK PART 1

BLUE STAR Valuation

Blue Star Valuation: About the Company

Blue Star is India's leading air conditioning and commercial refrigeration company. Its integrated business model of a manufacturer, contractor and after-sales service provider enables it to offer an end-to-end solution to its customers, which has proved to be a significant differentiator in the market place. The company mostly competes with other major players like Voltas operated by Tata Group and Lloyd operated by Havells in India. From here, we go ahead with Blue Star Valuation and Intrinsic Value of its shares.

Read more here: **Blue Star Shares Fundamental Analysis**

Methodology Used:

Discounted cash flow (DCF) is a valuation method used to estimate the value of an investment based on its expected future cash flows. DCF analysis attempts to figure out the value of an investment today, based on projections of how much money it will generate in the future. The following step by step procedure is followed.

1. Determining the Revenue Growth Rates
2. Forecasting the Financial Statements
3. Deriving the FCFF and FCFE
4. Calculating the Terminal Value
5. Calculating the Discount Rate
6. Discounting the Cashflows
7. Arriving at the Intrinsic Value of the Shares

Step 1: Determining the Revenue Growth Rates

We arrive at the below table by using the past and expected future performance of both the company and the economy. This along with adjustments to changes in the management expectations, extraordinary events and other macro factors give the revenue growth rates for Blue Star Valuation.

Financial Year	Revenue Growth Rate
Year 1	2%
Year 2	-16%
Year 3	27%
Year 4	13%
Year 5	13%

Revenue Growth Rates: Blue Star Valuation

Step 2: Forecasting the Financial Statements

The financial statements are forecasted for a period of 5 years using the annual report data of the company. The assumptions used for forecasting are tabulated below. The Excel model is completely editable and can be adjusted for specific changes which may happen over a period of time.

Assumptions Control Sheet	
Income Statement	
Average COGS as Percentage of Revenue	73.00%
Research and Development as Percentage of Revenue	0.00%
Sales, General and administrative as Percentage of Revenue	4.47%
Other operating expenses as Percentage of Revenue	15.00%
Other income (expense) as Percentage of Revenue	0.53%
Balance Sheet	
Short Term Debt as Percentage of Total Assets	11.49%
Long Term Debt as Percentage of Total Assets	0.70%
Cash and Cash Equivalents as Percentage of Revenue	1.54%
Short Term Equivalents as Percentage of Revenue	6.88%
Accounts Receivables as Percentage of Revenue	20.68%
Inventory as Percentage of Revenue	17.26%
Prepaid Expenses as Percentage of Revenue	1.72%
Other Current Assets as Percentage of Revenue	7.59%
Gross property, plant and equipment as Percentage of Revenue	7.58%
Intangible assets as Percentage of Revenue	1.28%
Other long-term assets as Percentage of Revenue	4.74%
Accounts payable as Percentage of Revenue	29.40%
Corporate Tax Rate	22.00%
Other current liabilities as Percentage of Revenue	11.66%
Retained Earnings as as Percentage of Net Income	33.86%
Accumulated other comprehensive income as Percentage of Revenue	7.88%
Cashflow Statement	
Other Working Capital as Percentage of Revenue	-0.57%

Financial Statements Forecast : Blue Star Valuation

Step 3: Deriving the FCFF and FCFE

Free cash flow to the firm (FCFF) represents the amount of cash flow from operations available for distribution after accounting for depreciation expenses, taxes, working capital, and investments. FCFF is a measurement of a company's profitability after all expenses and reinvestments. It is given as follows.

Free cash flow to equity (FCFE) is a measure of how much cash is available to the equity shareholders of a company after all expenses, reinvestment, and debt are paid. FCFE is a measure of equity capital usage.

F/S Items (INR Millions)	Mar-20	Mar-21	Mar-22	Mar-23	Mar-24

Free Cash Flow to Firm	3707	2481	3877	4047	4566
Free Cash Flow to Equity	4649	1979	4609	4500	5082

FCFF and FCFE values: Blue Star Valuation

Step 4: Calculating the Terminal Value

Terminal value (TV) is the value of a business or project beyond the forecast period when future cash flows can be estimated. It assumes that a business will grow at a set growth rate forever after the forecast period. Terminal value often comprises a large percentage of the total assessed value.

Terminal Value Calculation	Units INR Millions
Free Cash Flow to Firm	4565.82
Growth Rate	5.50%
Cost of Capital	14.45%
Terminal Value	53802.25

Terminal Value: Blue Star Valuation

Step 5: Calculating the Discount Rate

DCF analysis helps assess the viability of a project or investment by calculating the present value of expected future cash flows using a discount rate. Here we use the Weighted average cost of capital (WACC) to discount the cash flow. The below table from the excel model shows the calculation of WACC for Blue Star Valuation.

Cost of Equity Calcuation using CAPM	
Risk Free Rate (5 year G-Sec)	5.18%
Stock Beta (Ref: Reuters)	1.47
Beta Unlevered B/(1+ D(1-t)/E)	1.12
Beta Relevered B*(1+ D(1-t)/E)	1.49
Market Return Rm (Nifty 50 10 Year CAGR)	14.25%
Cost of Equity	**18.65%**

Cost of Debt	
Cost of Debt (Interest Expense/Total Debt)	4.35%

Cost of Capital	
Cost of Equity	18.65%
Weight of Equity in Target Capital Structure	70.66%
Cost of Debt	4.35%
Weight of Debt in Capital Structure	29.34%
WACC	**14.45%**

WACC Calculation for Blue Star Valuation.

Step 6: Discounting the Cashflows

The WACC and the Cost of Equity for the company calculated in the above step are then used to discount the FCFF, FCFE and Terminal Value calculated in Step 3 and 4. In our case, we'll only consider the FCFF based Intrinsic price of the shares as it represents the cash flow to all the suppliers of capital and not only to the equity shareholders. Thus we arrive at Present value of future FCFF for Blue Star Valuation. (Units are INR Millions)

FCFF Calculation	FV	Discounted
Mar-20	3707.27	3239.12
Mar-21	2481.16	1894.09
Mar-22	3876.52	2585.59
Mar-23	4047.17	2358.53
Mar-24	4565.82	2324.78
Terminal Value	53802.25	27394.52
Present Value (PV)		39796.63

FCFE Calculation	FV	Discounted
Mar-20	4649.27	3918.49
Mar-21	1978.54	1405.44
Mar-22	4609.25	2759.51
Mar-23	4500.34	2270.81
Mar-24	5082.01	2161.25
Terminal Value	53802.25	22880.70
Present Value (PV)		35396.19

PV of FCFF and FCFE for Blue Star Valuation.

Step 7: Arriving at the Intrinsic Value of the Shares

Dividing the PV of the FCFF and Terminal Value (the Value of the entire firm) by the number of outstanding shares we get the per share intrinsic value. We can compare this price with the current market price of the stock to get the Discount or Premium to its intrinsic price.

Blue Star Valuation	Units
PV in INR Million	39797
No of Shares Outstanding (In Million)	96

Intrinsic Value	414.55
Current Market Price of Share	658.00
Current Discount/Premium	59%

Intrinsic Value of the Shares: Blue Star Valuation

Blue Star Valuation and Intrinsic Share Price = INR 414.55

Divi's Labs Valuation

Divi's Labs Valuation: About the Company

Divi's Labs has been established for more than 29 years in Hyderabad with two manufacturing units and is among the top pharmaceuticals companies in India. The company is a leading manufacturer of APIs (Active pharmaceuticals ingredients), Intermediates and Registered starting materials offering high-quality products in over 95+ countries. The company is also known for its clientele network which includes some of the largest pharmaceutical companies in the world. From here, we go ahead with Divi's Labs Valuation and Intrinsic Value of its shares.

Read more here: Divi's Labs Shares Fundamental Analysis

Methodology Used:

Discounted cash flow (DCF) is a valuation method used to estimate the value of an investment based on its expected future cash flows. DCF analysis attempts to figure out the value of an investment today, based on projections of how much money it will generate in the future. The following step by step procedure is followed.

1. Determining the Revenue Growth Rates
2. Forecasting the Financial Statements
3. Deriving the FCFF and FCFE
4. Calculating the Terminal Value
5. Calculating the Discount Rate
6. Discounting the Cashflows
7. Arriving at the Intrinsic Value of the Shares

Step 1: Determining the Revenue Growth Rates

We arrive at the below table by using the past and expected future performance of both the company and the economy. This along with adjustments to changes in the management expectations, extraordinary events and other macro factors give the revenue growth rates for Divi's Labs Valuation.

Financial Year	Revenue Growth Rate

Year 1	8%
Year 2	28%
Year 3	19%
Year 4	16%
Year 5	15%

Revenue Growth Rates: Divi's Labs Valuation

Step 2: Forecasting the Financial Statements

The financial statements are forecasted for a period of 5 years using the annual report data of the company. The assumptions used for forecasting are tabulated below. The Excel model is completely editable and can be adjusted for specific changes which may happen over a period of time.

Assumptions Control Sheet	
Income Statement	
Average COGS as Percentage of Revenue	38.45%
Research and Development as Percentage of Revenue	0.46%
Sales, General and administrative as Percentage of Revenue	1.51%
Other operating expenses as Percentage of Revenue	26.52%
Other income (expense) as Percentage of Revenue	2.07%
Balance Sheet	
Short Term Debt as Percentage of Total Assets	0.90%
Long Term Debt as Percentage of Total Assets	0.00%
Cash and Cash Equivalents as Percentage of Revenue	0.48%
Short Term Equivalents as Percentage of Revenue	32.64%
Accounts Receivables as Percentage of Revenue	23.75%
Inventory as Percentage of Revenue	34.42%
Prepaid Expenses as Percentage of Revenue	1.01%
Other Current Assets as Percentage of Revenue	3.67%
Gross property, plant and equipment as Percentage of Revenue	62.88%
Intangible assets as Percentage of Revenue	0.11%
Other long-term assets as Percentage of Revenue	6.70%
Accounts payable as Percentage of Revenue	9.14%
Corporate Tax Rate	22.00%
Other current liabilities as Percentage of Revenue	5.22%
Retained Earnings as as Percentage of Net Income	66.17%
Accumulated other comprehensive income as Percentage of Revenue	27.20%
Cashflow Statement	
Other Working Capital as Percentage of Revenue	1.03%

Financial Statements Forecast : Divi's Labs Valuation

Step 3: Deriving the FCFF and FCFE

Free cash flow to the firm (FCFF) represents the amount of cash flow from operations available for distribution after accounting for depreciation expenses, taxes, working capital, and investments. FCFF is a measurement of a company's profitability after all expenses and reinvestments. It is given as follows.

Free cash flow to equity (FCFE) is a measure of how much cash is available to the equity shareholders of a company after all expenses, reinvestment, and debt are paid. FCFE is a measure of equity capital usage.

F/S Items (INR Millions)	Mar-20	Mar-21	Mar-22	Mar-23	Mar-24
Free Cash Flow to Firm	19241	18807	24482	28902	33416
Free Cash Flow to Equity	19056	18985	24680	29123	33662

FCFF and FCFE values: Divi's Labs Valuation

Step 4: Calculating the Terminal Value

Terminal value (TV) is the value of a business or project beyond the forecast period when future cash flows can be estimated. It assumes that a business will grow at a set growth rate forever after the forecast period. Terminal value often comprises a large percentage of the total assessed value.

Terminal Value Calculation	Units INR Millions
Free Cash Flow to Firm	33416.01
Growth Rate	5.00%
Cost of Capital	8.47%
Terminal Value	1012084.56

Terminal Value: Divi's Labs Valuation

Step 5: Calculating the Discount Rate

DCF analysis helps assess the viability of a project or investment by calculating the present value of expected future cash flows using a discount rate. Here we use the Weighted average cost of capital (WACC) to discount the cash flow. The below table from

the excel model shows the calculation of WACC for Divi's Labs Valuation.

Cost of Equity Calcuation using CAPM	
Risk Free Rate (5 year G-Sec)	5.18%
Stock Beta (Ref: Reuters)	0.37
Beta Unlevered B/(1+ D(1-t)/E)	0.37
Beta Relevered B*(1+ D(1-t)/E)	0.37
Market Return Rm (Nifty 50 10 Year CAGR)	14.25%
Cost of Equity	**8.52%**

Cost of Debt	
Cost of Debt (Interest Expense/Total Debt)	**3.00%**

Cost of Capital	
Cost of Equity	8.52%
Weight of Equity in Target Capital Structure	98.97%
Cost of Debt	3.00%
Weight of Debt in Capital Structure	1.03%
WACC	**8.47%**

WACC Calculation for Divi's Labs Valuation.

Step 6: Discounting the Cashflows

The WACC and the Cost of Equity for the company calculated in the above step are then used to discount the FCFF, FCFE and Terminal Value calculated in Step 3 and 4. In our case, we'll only consider the FCFF based Intrinsic price of the shares as it represents the cash flow to all the suppliers of capital and not only to the equity shareholders. Thus we arrive at Present value of future FCFF for Divi's Labs Valuation. (Units are INR Millions)

STOCK VALUATION HANDBOOK PART 1

FCFF Calculation	FV	Discounted
Mar-20	19240.57	17738.67
Mar-21	18807.19	15985.65
Mar-22	24482.19	19184.92
Mar-23	28902.40	20880.78
Mar-24	33416.01	22257.21
Terminal Value	1012084.56	674113.34
Present Value (PV)		770160.58

FCFE Calculation	FV	Discounted
Mar-20	19055.57	17558.95
Mar-21	18985.23	16120.13
Mar-22	24680.11	19309.74
Mar-23	29122.65	20996.00
Mar-24	33662.01	22362.59
Terminal Value	1012084.56	672355.46
Present Value (PV)		768702.87

PV of FCFF and FCFE for Divi's Labs Valuation.

Step 7: Arriving at the Intrinsic Value of the Shares

Dividing the PV of the FCFF and Terminal Value (the Value of the entire firm) by the number of outstanding shares we get the per share intrinsic value. We can compare this price with the current market price of the stock to get the Discount or Premium to its intrinsic price.

Divi's Labs Valuation	Units
PV in INR Million	770161
No of Shares Outstanding (In Million)	265

Intrinsic Value	2906.27
Current Market Price of Share	3358.00
Current Discount/Premium	16%

Intrinsic Value of the Shares: Divi's Labs Valuation

Divi's Labs Valuation and Intrinsic Share Price = INR 2906.27

BHARAT PETROLEUM VALUATION

Bharat Petroleum Valuation: About the Company

The company today known as BPCL started off as Rangoon Oil and Exploration company set up during the British colonial rule of India. Bharat Petroleum was incorporated in 1976, when Bharat Refineries, a 100% public sector enterprise of the Indian Government acquired the complete ownership of Burmah Shell Company's assets in India. Today, BPCL is India's 2nd largest downstream oil company and is ranked 275th on the Fortune list of the world's biggest corporations. From here, we go ahead with Bharat Petroleum Valuation and Intrinsic Value of its shares.

Read more here: **Bharat Petroleum Shares Fundamental Analysis**

Methodology Used:

Discounted cash flow (DCF) is a valuation method used to estimate the value of an investment based on its expected future cash flows. DCF analysis attempts to figure out the value of an investment today, based on projections of how much money it will generate in the future. The following step by step procedure is followed.

1. Determining the Revenue Growth Rates
2. Forecasting the Financial Statements
3. Deriving the FCFF and FCFE
4. Calculating the Terminal Value
5. Calculating the Discount Rate
6. Discounting the Cashflows
7. Arriving at the Intrinsic Value of the Shares

Step 1: Determining the Revenue Growth Rates

We arrive at the below table by using the past and expected future performance of both the company and the economy. This along with adjustments to changes in the management expectations, extraordinary events and other macro factors give the revenue growth rates for Bharat Petroleum Valuation.

Financial Year	Revenue Growth Rate
Year 1	-5%
Year 2	-25%
Year 3	16%
Year 4	14%
Year 5	14%

Revenue Growth Rates: Bharat Petroleum Valuation

Step 2: Forecasting the Financial Statements

The financial statements are forecasted for a period of 5 years using the annual report data of the company. The assumptions used for forecasting are tabulated below. The Excel model is completely editable and can be adjusted for specific changes which may happen over a period of time.

Assumptions Control Sheet	
Income Statement	
Average COGS as Percentage of Revenue	89.73%
Research and Development as Percentage of Revenue	0.00%
Sales, General and administrative as Percentage of Revenue	0.43%
Other operating expenses as Percentage of Revenue	5.47%
Other income (expense) as Percentage of Revenue	1.23%
Balance Sheet	
Short Term Debt as Percentage of Total Assets	7.28%
Long Term Debt as Percentage of Total Assets	23.03%
Cash and Cash Equivalents as Percentage of Revenue	0.89%
Short Term Equivalents as Percentage of Revenue	2.47%
Accounts Receivables as Percentage of Revenue	1.77%
Inventory as Percentage of Revenue	8.40%
Prepaid Expenses as Percentage of Revenue	0.46%
Other Current Assets as Percentage of Revenue	2.65%
Gross property, plant and equipment as Percentage of Revenue	20.89%
Intangible assets as Percentage of Revenue	2.27%
Other long-term assets as Percentage of Revenue	8.03%
Accounts payable as Percentage of Revenue	5.68%
Corporate Tax Rate	22.00%
Other current liabilities as Percentage of Revenue	8.61%
Retained Earnings as as Percentage of Net Income	6.25%
Accumulated other comprehensive income as Percentage of Revenue	12.45%
Cashflow Statement	
Other Working Capital as Percentage of Revenue	-0.67%

Financial Statements Forecast : Bharat Petroleum Valuation

Step 3: Deriving the FCFF and FCFE

Free cash flow to the firm (FCFF) represents the amount of cash flow from operations available for distribution after accounting for depreciation expenses, taxes, working capital, and investments. FCFF is a measurement of a company's profitability after all expenses and reinvestments. It is given as follows.

Free cash flow to equity (FCFE) is a measure of how much cash is available to the equity shareholders of a company after all expenses, reinvestment, and debt are paid. FCFE is a measure of equity capital usage.

F/S Items (INR Millions)	Mar-20	Mar-21	Mar-22	Mar-23	Mar-24

Free Cash Flow to Firm	143908	47122	94555	114055	124760
Free Cash Flow to Equity	53942	-36885	86716	104257	178581

FCFF and FCFE values: Bharat Petroleum Valuation

Step 4: Calculating the Terminal Value

Terminal value (TV) is the value of a business or project beyond the forecast period when future cash flows can be estimated. It assumes that a business will grow at a set growth rate forever after the forecast period. Terminal value often comprises a large percentage of the total assessed value.

Terminal Value Calculation	Units INR Millions
Free Cash Flow to Firm	124760.04
Growth Rate	4.00%
Cost of Capital	13.32%
Terminal Value	1392249.59

Terminal Value: Bharat Petroleum Valuation

Step 5: Calculating the Discount Rate

DCF analysis helps assess the viability of a project or investment by calculating the present value of expected future cash flows using a discount rate. Here we use the Weighted average cost of capital (WACC) to discount the cash flow. The below table from the excel model shows the calculation of WACC for Bharat Petroleum Valuation.

Cost of Equity Calcuation using CAPM	
Risk Free Rate (5 year G-Sec)	5.18%
Stock Beta (Ref: Reuters)	1.29
Beta Unlevered B/(1+ D(1-t)/E)	0.68
Beta Relevered B*(1+ D(1-t)/E)	1.30
Market Return Rm (Nifty 50 10 Year CAGR)	14.25%
Cost of Equity	**16.99%**

Cost of Debt	
Cost of Debt (Interest Expense/Total Debt)	10.21%

Cost of Capital	
Cost of Equity	16.99%
Weight of Equity in Target Capital Structure	45.89%
Cost of Debt	10.21%
Weight of Debt in Capital Structure	54.11%
WACC	**13.32%**

WACC Calculation for Bharat Petroleum Valuation.

Step 6: Discounting the Cashflows

The WACC and the Cost of Equity for the company calculated in the above step are then used to discount the FCFF, FCFE and Terminal Value calculated in Step 3 and 4. In our case, we'll only consider the FCFF based Intrinsic price of the shares as it represents the cash flow to all the suppliers of capital and not only to the equity shareholders. Thus we arrive at Present value of future FCFF for Bharat Petroleum Valuation. (Units are INR Millions)

FCFF Calculation	FV	Discounted
Mar-20	143907.74	126992.94
Mar-21	47121.60	36695.33
Mar-22	94554.82	64978.54
Mar-23	114054.61	69166.30
Mar-24	124760.04	66765.58
Terminal Value	1392249.59	745065.08
Present Value (PV)		1109663.77

FCFE Calculation	FV	Discounted
Mar-20	53941.66	46109.17
Mar-21	-36884.85	-26950.95
Mar-22	86715.55	54160.92
Mar-23	104256.70	55661.64
Mar-24	178580.53	81498.41
Terminal Value	1392249.59	635377.97
Present Value (PV)		845857.16

PV of FCFF and FCFE for Bharat Petroleum Valuation.

Step 7: Arriving at the Intrinsic Value of the Shares

Dividing the PV of the FCFF and Terminal Value (the Value of the entire firm) by the number of outstanding shares we get the per share intrinsic value. We can compare this price with the current market price of the stock to get the Discount or Premium to its intrinsic price.

Bharat Petroleum Valuation	Units
PV in INR Million	1109664
No of Shares Outstanding (In Million)	1967

Intrinsic Value	564.14
Current Market Price of Share	374.00
Current Discount/Premium	-34%

Intrinsic Value of the Shares: Bharat Petroleum Valuation

Bharat Petroleum Valuation and Intrinsic Share Price = INR 564.14

CROMPTON GREAVES VALUATION

Crompton Greaves Valuation

Crompton Greaves Valuation: About the Company

Crompton Greaves competes with some leading companies like Anchor, Havells and Polycab in the Indian market. The industry structure is asset-heavy and therefore requires intensive investments in Plant, Property and Equipment. So the threat of new competition from outside is less. The company is focused on premiumization and branding which gives it some competitive advantage over others, but this is not sustainable as it can be easily copied by the competitors. Therefore this category gets only 2 stars in Crompton Greaves shares fundamental analysis. From here, we go ahead with Crompton Greaves Valuation and Intrinsic Value of its shares.

Read more here: **Crompton Greaves Shares Fundamental Analysis**

Methodology Used:

Discounted cash flow (DCF) is a valuation method used to estimate the value of an investment based on its expected future cash flows. DCF analysis attempts to figure out the value of an investment today, based on projections of how much money it will generate in the future. The following step by step procedure is followed.

1. Determining the Revenue Growth Rates
2. Forecasting the Financial Statements
3. Deriving the FCFF and FCFE
4. Calculating the Terminal Value
5. Calculating the Discount Rate
6. Discounting the Cashflows
7. Arriving at the Intrinsic Value of the Shares

Step 1: Determining the Revenue Growth Rates

We arrive at the below table by using the past and expected future performance of both the company and the economy. This along with adjustments to changes in the management expectations, extraordinary events and other macro factors give the revenue growth rates for Crompton Greaves Valuation.

Financial Year	Revenue Growth Rate
Year 1	1%
Year 2	-2%
Year 3	16%
Year 4	14%
Year 5	14%

Revenue Growth Rates: Crompton Greaves Valuation

Step 2: Forecasting the Financial Statements

The financial statements are forecasted for a period of 5 years using the annual report data of the company. The assumptions used for forecasting are tabulated below. The Excel model is completely editable and can be adjusted for specific changes which may happen over a period of time.

Assumptions Control Sheet	
Income Statement	
Average COGS as Percentage of Revenue	69.74%
Research and Development as Percentage of Revenue	0.00%
Sales, General and administrative as Percentage of Revenue	8.75%
Other operating expenses as Percentage of Revenue	9.03%
Other income (expense) as Percentage of Revenue	0.42%
Balance Sheet	
Short Term Debt as Percentage of Total Assets	9.10%
Long Term Debt as Percentage of Total Assets	25.27%
Cash and Cash Equivalents as Percentage of Revenue	3.00%
Short Term Equivalents as Percentage of Revenue	11.75%
Accounts Receivables as Percentage of Revenue	12.93%
Inventory as Percentage of Revenue	7.96%
Prepaid Expenses as Percentage of Revenue	0.77%
Other Current Assets as Percentage of Revenue	1.62%
Gross property, plant and equipment as Percentage of Revenue	2.48%
Intangible assets as Percentage of Revenue	0.13%
Other long-term assets as Percentage of Revenue	0.60%
Accounts payable as Percentage of Revenue	19.51%
Corporate Tax Rate	22.00%
Other current liabilities as Percentage of Revenue	4.97%
Retained Earnings as as Percentage of Net Income	48.36%
Accumulated other comprehensive income as Percentage of Revenue	1.76%
Cashflow Statement	
Other Working Capital as Percentage of Revenue	-0.06%

Financial Statements Forecast : Crompton Greaves Valuation

Step 3: Deriving the FCFF and FCFE

Free cash flow to the firm (FCFF) represents the amount of cash flow from operations available for distribution after accounting for depreciation expenses, taxes, working capital, and investments. FCFF is a measurement of a company's profitability after all expenses and reinvestments. It is given as follows.

Free cash flow to equity (FCFE) is a measure of how much cash is available to the equity shareholders of a company after all expenses, reinvestment, and debt are paid. FCFE is a measure of equity capital usage.

F/S Items (INR Millions)	Mar-20	Mar-21	Mar-22	Mar-23	Mar-24
Free Cash Flow to Firm	3946	3658	4197	5055	6140
Free Cash Flow to Equity	9717	3593	5304	6239	7544

FCFF and FCFE values: Crompton Greaves Valuation

Step 4: Calculating the Terminal Value

Terminal value (TV) is the value of a business or project beyond the forecast period when future cash flows can be estimated. It assumes that a business will grow at a set growth rate forever after the forecast period. Terminal value often comprises a large percentage of the total assessed value.

Terminal Value Calculation	Units INR Millions
Free Cash Flow to Firm	6140.28
Growth Rate	5.00%
Cost of Capital	10.98%
Terminal Value	107803.57

Terminal Value: Crompton Greaves Valuation

Step 5: Calculating the Discount Rate

DCF analysis helps assess the viability of a project or investment by calculating the present value of expected future cash flows using a discount rate. Here we use the Weighted average cost of capital (WACC) to discount the cash flow. The below table from

the excel model shows the calculation of WACC for Crompton Greaves Valuation.

Cost of Equity Calcuation using CAPM	
Risk Free Rate (5 year G-Sec)	5.18%
Stock Beta (Ref: Reuters)	0.85
Beta Unlevered B/(1+ D(1-t)/E)	0.58
Beta Relevered B*(1+ D(1-t)/E)	1.02
Market Return Rm (Nifty 50 10 Year CAGR)	14.25%
Cost of Equity	**14.42%**

Cost of Debt	
Cost of Debt (Interest Expense/Total Debt)	7.41%

Cost of Capital	
Cost of Equity	14.42%
Weight of Equity in Target Capital Structure	50.95%
Cost of Debt	7.41%
Weight of Debt in Capital Structure	49.05%
WACC	**10.98%**

WACC Calculation for Crompton Greaves Valuation.

Step 6: Discounting the Cashflows

The WACC and the Cost of Equity for the company calculated in the above step are then used to discount the FCFF, FCFE and Terminal Value calculated in Step 3 and 4. In our case, we'll only consider the FCFF based Intrinsic price of the shares as it represents the cash flow to all the suppliers of capital and not only to the equity shareholders. Thus we arrive at Present value of future FCFF for Crompton Greaves Valuation. (Units are INR Millions)

STOCK VALUATION HANDBOOK PART 1

FCFF Calculation	FV	Discounted
Mar-20	3946.10	3555.67
Mar-21	3658.24	2970.15
Mar-22	4197.22	3070.58
Mar-23	5055.11	3332.29
Mar-24	6140.28	3647.14
Terminal Value	107803.57	64032.12
Present Value (PV)		**80607.96**

FCFE Calculation	FV	Discounted
Mar-20	9716.95	8492.60
Mar-21	3592.71	2744.38
Mar-22	5303.66	3540.85
Mar-23	6238.97	3640.46
Mar-24	7543.58	3847.08
Terminal Value	107803.57	54977.77
Present Value (PV)		**77243.15**

PV of FCFF and FCFE for Crompton Greaves Valuation.

Step 7: Arriving at the Intrinsic Value of the Shares

Dividing the PV of the FCFF and Terminal Value (the Value of the entire firm) by the number of outstanding shares we get the per share intrinsic value. We can compare this price with the current market price of the stock to get the Discount or Premium to its intrinsic price.

Crompton Greaves Valuation	Units
PV in INR Million	80608
No of Shares Outstanding (In Million)	627

Intrinsic Value	128.56
Current Market Price of Share	296.00
Current Discount/Premium	130%

Intrinsic Value of the Shares: Crompton Greaves Valuation

Crompton Greaves Valuation and Intrinsic Share Price = INR 128.56

ESCORTS VALUATION

Escorts Valuation: About the Company

Escorts is an automotive engineering company that operates in the sectors of agri-machinery, construction and material handling equipment, and railway equipment. It was established in 1944 and since then it has grown through multiples collaborations and Joint Ventures with companies like JCB, Doosan and Tadano. Escorts is headquartered in Faridabad and has marketing operations in 40+ countries. From here, we go ahead with Escorts Valuation and Intrinsic Value of its shares.

Read more here: **Escorts Shares Fundamental Analysis**

Methodology Used:

Discounted cash flow (DCF) is a valuation method used to estimate the value of an investment based on its expected future cash flows. DCF analysis attempts to figure out the value of an investment today, based on projections of how much money it will generate in the future. The following step by step procedure is followed.

1. Determining the Revenue Growth Rates
2. Forecasting the Financial Statements
3. Deriving the FCFF and FCFE
4. Calculating the Terminal Value
5. Calculating the Discount Rate
6. Discounting the Cashflows
7. Arriving at the Intrinsic Value of the Shares

Step 1: Determining the Revenue Growth Rates

We arrive at the below table by using the past and expected future performance of both the company and the economy. This along with adjustments to changes in the management expectations, extraordinary events and other macro factors give the revenue growth rates for Escorts Valuation.

Financial Year	Revenue Growth Rate
Year 1	-9%
Year 2	10%
Year 3	15%
Year 4	14%
Year 5	13%

Revenue Growth Rates: Escorts Valuation

Step 2: Forecasting the Financial Statements

The financial statements are forecasted for a period of 5 years using the annual report data of the company. The assumptions used for forecasting are tabulated below. The Excel model is completely editable and can be adjusted for specific changes which may happen over a period of time.

Assumptions Control Sheet	
Income Statement	
Average COGS as Percentage of Revenue	70.18%
Research and Development as Percentage of Revenue	0.24%
Sales, General and administrative as Percentage of Revenue	5.24%
Other operating expenses as Percentage of Revenue	17.66%
Other income (expense) as Percentage of Revenue	1.10%
Balance Sheet	
Short Term Debt as Percentage of Total Assets	6.67%
Long Term Debt as Percentage of Total Assets	1.57%
Cash and Cash Equivalents as Percentage of Revenue	1.76%
Short Term Equivalents as Percentage of Revenue	5.91%
Accounts Receivables as Percentage of Revenue	11.87%
Inventory as Percentage of Revenue	12.03%
Prepaid Expenses as Percentage of Revenue	0.34%
Other Current Assets as Percentage of Revenue	6.61%
Gross property, plant and equipment as Percentage of Revenue	52.62%
Intangible assets as Percentage of Revenue	1.15%
Other long-term assets as Percentage of Revenue	3.17%
Accounts payable as Percentage of Revenue	17.69%
Corporate Tax Rate	22.00%
Other current liabilities as Percentage of Revenue	10.85%
Retained Earnings as as Percentage of Net Income	100.00%
Accumulated other comprehensive income as Percentage of Revenue	18.50%
Cashflow Statement	
Other Working Capital as Percentage of Revenue	1.95%

Financial Statements Forecast : Escorts Valuation

Step 3: Deriving the FCFF and FCFE

Free cash flow to the firm (FCFF) represents the amount of cash flow from operations available for distribution after accounting for depreciation expenses, taxes, working capital, and investments. FCFF is a measurement of a company's profitability after all expenses and reinvestments. It is given as follows.

Free cash flow to equity (FCFE) is a measure of how much cash is available to the equity shareholders of a company after all expenses, reinvestment, and debt are paid. FCFE is a measure of equity capital usage.

F/S Items (INR Millions)	Mar-20	Mar-21	Mar-22	Mar-23	Mar-24
Free Cash Flow to Firm	-1776	2517	4407	4743	5049
Free Cash Flow to Equity	-86	2823	4853	5251	5640

FCFF and FCFE values: Escorts Valuation

Step 4: Calculating the Terminal Value

Terminal value (TV) is the value of a business or project beyond the forecast period when future cash flows can be estimated. It assumes that a business will grow at a set growth rate forever after the forecast period. Terminal value often comprises a large percentage of the total assessed value.

Terminal Value Calculation	Units INR Millions
Free Cash Flow to Firm	5049.03
Growth Rate	5.50%
Cost of Capital	14.66%
Terminal Value	58127.24

Terminal Value: Escorts Valuation

Step 5: Calculating the Discount Rate

DCF analysis helps assess the viability of a project or investment by calculating the present value of expected future cash flows using a discount rate. Here we use the Weighted average cost of capital (WACC) to discount the cash flow. The below table

from the excel model shows the calculation of WACC for Escorts Valuation.

Cost of Equity Calcuation using CAPM	
Risk Free Rate (5 year G-Sec)	5.18%
Stock Beta (Ref: Reuters)	1.15
Beta Unlevered B/(1+ D(1-t)/E)	1.06
Beta Relevered B*(1+ D(1-t)/E)	1.19
Market Return Rm (Nifty 50 10 Year CAGR)	14.25%
Cost of Equity	**16.00%**

Cost of Debt	
Cost of Debt (Interest Expense/Total Debt)	**6.15%**

Cost of Capital	
Cost of Equity	16.00%
Weight of Equity in Target Capital Structure	86.42%
Cost of Debt	6.15%
Weight of Debt in Capital Structure	13.58%
WACC	**14.66%**

WACC Calculation for Escorts Valuation.

Step 6: Discounting the Cashflows

The WACC and the Cost of Equity for the company calculated in the above step are then used to discount the FCFF, FCFE and Terminal Value calculated in Step 3 and 4. In our case, we'll only consider the FCFF based Intrinsic price of the shares as it represents the cash flow to all the suppliers of capital and not only to the equity shareholders. Thus we arrive at Present value of future FCFF for Escorts Valuation. (Units are INR Millions)

FCFF Calculation	FV	Discounted
Mar-20	-1776.09	-1548.95
Mar-21	2516.76	1914.21
Mar-22	4407.25	2923.40
Mar-23	4742.75	2743.62
Mar-24	5049.03	2547.27
Terminal Value	58127.24	29325.54
Present Value (PV)		37905.07

FCFE Calculation	FV	Discounted
Mar-20	-86.45	-74.52
Mar-21	2822.77	2097.70
Mar-22	4853.35	3109.17
Mar-23	5251.36	2900.08
Mar-24	5640.30	2685.19
Terminal Value	58127.24	27672.70
Present Value (PV)		38390.31

PV of FCFF and FCFE for Escorts Valuation.

Step 7: Arriving at the Intrinsic Value of the Shares

Dividing the PV of the FCFF and Terminal Value (the Value of the entire firm) by the number of outstanding shares we get the per share intrinsic value. We can compare this price with the current market price of the stock to get the Discount or Premium to its intrinsic price.

Escorts Valuation	Units
PV in INR Million	37905
No of Shares Outstanding (In Million)	86

Intrinsic Value	440.76
Current Market Price of Share	1358.00
Current Discount/Premium	208%

Intrinsic Value of the Shares: Escorts Valuation

Escorts Valuation and Intrinsic Share Price = INR 440.76

AVENUE SUPERMARTS VALUATION

Avenue Supermarts Valuation: About the Company

DMart was started by Mr Radhakishan Damani to address the growing needs of retail in India. From the launch of its first store in Powai in 2002, DMart today has a well-established presence in 214+ locations across 12+ states in India. The supermarket chain of DMart stores is owned and operated by Avenue Supermarts Ltd. (ASL) which is headquartered in Mumbai. From here, we go ahead with Avenue Supermarts Valuation and Intrinsic Value of its shares.

Read more here: **Avenue Supermarts Shares Fundamental Analysis**

Methodology Used:

Discounted cash flow (DCF) is a valuation method used to estimate the value of an investment based on its expected future cash flows. DCF analysis attempts to figure out the value of an investment today, based on projections of how much money it will generate in the future. The following step by step procedure is followed.

1. Determining the Revenue Growth Rates
2. Forecasting the Financial Statements
3. Deriving the FCFF and FCFE
4. Calculating the Terminal Value
5. Calculating the Discount Rate
6. Discounting the Cashflows
7. Arriving at the Intrinsic Value of the Shares

Step 1: Determining the Revenue Growth Rates

We arrive at the below table by using the past and expected future performance of both the company and the economy. This along with adjustments to changes in the management expectations, extraordinary events and other macro factors give the revenue growth rates for Avenue Supermarts Valuation.

Financial Year	Revenue Growth Rate

Year 1	24%
Year 2	-3%
Year 3	40%
Year 4	29%
Year 5	35%

Revenue Growth Rates: Avenue Supermarts Valuation

Step 2: Forecasting the Financial Statements

The financial statements are forecasted for a period of 5 years using the annual report data of the company. The assumptions used for forecasting are tabulated below. The Excel model is completely editable and can be adjusted for specific changes which may happen over a period of time.

Assumptions Control Sheet	
Income Statement	
Average COGS as Percentage of Revenue	84.95%
Research and Development as Percentage of Revenue	0.00%
Sales, General and administrative as Percentage of Revenue	0.20%
Other operating expenses as Percentage of Revenue	7.74%
Other income (expense) as Percentage of Revenue	0.29%
Balance Sheet	
Short Term Debt as Percentage of Total Assets	7.34%
Long Term Debt as Percentage of Total Assets	12.43%
Cash and Cash Equivalents as Percentage of Revenue	0.48%
Short Term Equivalents as Percentage of Revenue	4.03%
Accounts Receivables as Percentage of Revenue	0.22%
Inventory as Percentage of Revenue	7.95%
Prepaid Expenses as Percentage of Revenue	0.78%
Other Current Assets as Percentage of Revenue	0.19%
Gross property, plant and equipment as Percentage of Revenue	25.54%
Intangible assets as Percentage of Revenue	0.13%
Other long-term assets as Percentage of Revenue	1.08%
Accounts payable as Percentage of Revenue	2.19%
Corporate Tax Rate	22.00%
Other current liabilities as Percentage of Revenue	1.07%
Retained Earnings as as Percentage of Net Income	102.88%
Accumulated other comprehensive income as Percentage of Revenue	0.59%
Cashflow Statement	
Other Working Capital as Percentage of Revenue	-0.23%

Financial Statements Forecast : Avenue Supermarts Valuation

Step 3: Deriving the FCFF and FCFE

Free cash flow to the firm (FCFF) represents the amount of cash flow from operations available for distribution after accounting for depreciation expenses, taxes, working capital, and investments. FCFF is a measurement of a company's profitability after all expenses and reinvestments. It is given as follows.

Free cash flow to equity (FCFE) is a measure of how much cash is available to the equity shareholders of a company after all expenses, reinvestment, and debt are paid. FCFE is a measure of equity capital usage.

F/S Items (INR Millions)	Mar-20	Mar-21	Mar-22	Mar-23	Mar-24
Free Cash Flow to Firm	5999	3024	12216	18642	31270
Free Cash Flow to Equity	18339	5031	16771	24477	39887

FCFF and FCFE values: Avenue Supermarts Valuation

Step 4: Calculating the Terminal Value

Terminal value (TV) is the value of a business or project beyond the forecast period when future cash flows can be estimated. It assumes that a business will grow at a set growth rate forever after the forecast period. Terminal value often comprises a large percentage of the total assessed value.

Terminal Value Calculation	Units INR Millions
Free Cash Flow to Firm	31270.01
Growth Rate	6.00%
Cost of Capital	7.85%
Terminal Value	1790294.61

Terminal Value: Avenue Supermarts Valuation

Step 5: Calculating the Discount Rate

DCF analysis helps assess the viability of a project or investment by calculating the present value of expected future cash flows using a discount rate. Here we use the Weighted average cost of capital (WACC) to discount the cash flow. The below table

from the excel model shows the calculation of WACC for Avenue Supermarts Valuation.

Cost of Equity Calcuation using CAPM	
Risk Free Rate (5 year G-Sec)	5.18%
Stock Beta (Ref: Reuters)	0.30
Beta Unlevered B/(1+ D(1-t)/E)	0.27
Beta Relevered B*(1+ D(1-t)/E)	0.33
Market Return Rm (Nifty 50 10 Year CAGR)	14.25%
Cost of Equity	**8.16%**

Cost of Debt	
Cost of Debt (Interest Expense/Total Debt)	6.59%

Cost of Capital	
Cost of Equity	8.16%
Weight of Equity in Target Capital Structure	79.42%
Cost of Debt	6.59%
Weight of Debt in Capital Structure	20.58%
WACC	**7.84%**

WACC Calculation for Avenue Supermarts Valuation.

Step 6: Discounting the Cashflows

The WACC and the Cost of Equity for the company calculated in the above step are then used to discount the FCFF, FCFE and Terminal Value calculated in Step 3 and 4. In our case, we'll only consider the FCFF based Intrinsic price of the shares as it represents the cash flow to all the suppliers of capital and not only to the equity shareholders. Thus we arrive at Present value of future FCFF for Avenue Supermarts Valuation. (Units are INR Millions)

BILLION DOLLAR VALUATION

FCFF Calculation	FV	Discounted
Mar-20	6025.22	5587.40
Mar-21	3103.70	2669.03
Mar-22	12279.38	9792.35
Mar-23	18712.02	13837.84
Mar-24	31336.36	21489.83
Terminal Value	1809338.87	1240807.23
Present Value (PV)		1294183.68

FCFE Calculation	FV	Discounted
Mar-20	16659.00	15402.23
Mar-21	1711.36	1462.89
Mar-22	18168.87	14359.26
Mar-23	24334.45	17781.16
Mar-24	40439.39	27319.82
Terminal Value	1809338.87	1222343.22
Present Value (PV)		1298668.57

PV of FCFF and FCFE for Avenue Supermarts Valuation.

Step 7: Arriving at the Intrinsic Value of the Shares

Dividing the PV of the FCFF and Terminal Value (the Value of the entire firm) by the number of outstanding shares we get the per share intrinsic value. We can compare this price with the current market price of the stock to get the Discount or Premium to its intrinsic price.

Avenue Supermarts Valuation	Units
PV in INR Million	1279966
No of Shares Outstanding (In Million)	624
Intrinsic Value	2051.23

Current Market Price of Share	2398.00
Current Discount/Premium	17%

Intrinsic Value of the Shares: Avenue Supermarts Valuation

Avenue Supermarts Valuation and Intrinsic Share Price = INR 2051.23

CEAT SHARES VALUATION

CEAT Shares Valuation: About the Company

CEAT was established in 1958 and is a flagship company of INR 220 billion RPG Enterprises. Today, CEAT is one of India's leading tyre manufacturers and has a strong presence in global markets. The company produces over 15+ million tyres a year. CEAT manufactures radial tyres for heavy-duty trucks and buses, light commercial vehicles, earthmovers, forklifts, tractors, trailers, cars, motorcycles and scooters as well as auto-rickshaws.. The company has also been ranked as 34th best brand in India. From here, we go ahead with CEAT Shares Valuation and Intrinsic Value of its shares.

Read more here: CEAT Shares Fundamental Analysis

Methodology Used:

Discounted cash flow (DCF) is a valuation method used to estimate the value of an investment based on its expected future cash flows. DCF analysis attempts to figure out the value of an investment today, based on projections of how much money it will generate in the future. The following step by step procedure is followed.

1. Determining the Revenue Growth Rates
2. Forecasting the Financial Statements
3. Deriving the FCFF and FCFE
4. Calculating the Terminal Value
5. Calculating the Discount Rate
6. Discounting the Cashflows
7. Arriving at the Intrinsic Value of the Shares

Step 1: Determining the Revenue Growth Rates

We arrive at the below table by using the past and expected future performance of both the company and the economy. This along with adjustments to changes in the management expectations, extraordinary events and other macro factors give the revenue growth rates for CEAT Shares Valuation.

Financial Year	Revenue Growth Rate
Year 1	-3%
Year 2	-1%
Year 3	15%
Year 4	11%
Year 5	10%

Revenue Growth Rates: CEAT Shares Valuation

Step 2: Forecasting the Financial Statements

The financial statements are forecasted for a period of 5 years using the annual report data of the company. The assumptions used for forecasting are tabulated below. The Excel model is completely editable and can be adjusted for specific changes which may happen over a period of time.

Assumptions Control Sheet	
Income Statement	
Average COGS as Percentage of Revenue	60.50%
Research and Development as Percentage of Revenue	0.00%
Sales, General and administrative as Percentage of Revenue	8.26%
Other operating expenses as Percentage of Revenue	22.02%
Other income (expense) as Percentage of Revenue	-0.05%
Balance Sheet	
Short Term Debt as Percentage of Total Assets	5.15%
Long Term Debt as Percentage of Total Assets	14.23%
Cash and Cash Equivalents as Percentage of Revenue	1.10%
Short Term Equivalents as Percentage of Revenue	1.52%
Accounts Receivables as Percentage of Revenue	11.05%
Inventory as Percentage of Revenue	13.34%
Prepaid Expenses as Percentage of Revenue	0.83%
Other Current Assets as Percentage of Revenue	1.93%
Gross property, plant and equipment as Percentage of Revenue	48.82%
Intangible assets as Percentage of Revenue	1.26%
Other long-term assets as Percentage of Revenue	4.99%
Accounts payable as Percentage of Revenue	13.11%
Corporate Tax Rate	22.00%
Other current liabilities as Percentage of Revenue	9.18%
Retained Earnings as as Percentage of Net Income	76.61%
Accumulated other comprehensive income as Percentage of Revenue	3.98%
Cashflow Statement	
Other Working Capital as Percentage of Revenue	-1.71%

Financial Statements Forecast :CEAT Shares Valuation

Step 3: Deriving the FCFF and FCFE

Free cash flow to the firm (FCFF) represents the amount of cash flow from operations available for distribution after accounting for depreciation expenses, taxes, working capital, and investments. FCFF is a measurement of a company's profitability after all expenses and reinvestments. It is given as follows.

Free cash flow to equity (FCFE) is a measure of how much cash is available to the equity shareholders of a company after all expenses, reinvestment, and debt are paid. FCFE is a measure of equity capital usage.

F/S Items (INR Millions)	Mar-20	Mar-21	Mar-22	Mar-23	Mar-24
Free Cash Flow to Firm	4994	1181	1643	1797	2031
Free Cash Flow to Equity	993	958	2082	2139	2364

FCFF and FCFE values: CEAT Shares Valuation

Step 4: Calculating the Terminal Value

Terminal value (TV) is the value of a business or project beyond the forecast period when future cash flows can be estimated. It assumes that a business will grow at a set growth rate forever after the forecast period. Terminal value often comprises a large percentage of the total assessed value.

Terminal Value Calculation	Units INR Millions
Free Cash Flow to Firm	2030.79
Growth Rate	5.00%
Cost of Capital	10.36%
Terminal Value	39795.80

Terminal Value: CEAT Shares Valuation

Step 5: Calculating the Discount Rate

DCF analysis helps assess the viability of a project or investment by calculating the present value of expected future cash flows using a discount rate. Here we use the Weighted average cost of capital (WACC) to discount the cash flow. The below table from

the excel model shows the calculation of WACC for Ashok Leyland Valuation.

Cost of Equity Calcuation using CAPM	
Risk Free Rate (5 year G-Sec)	5.18%
Stock Beta (Ref: Reuters)	0.67
Beta Unlevered B/(1+ D(1-t)/E)	0.47
Beta Relevered B*(1+ D(1-t)/E)	0.61
Market Return Rm (Nifty 50 10 Year CAGR)	14.25%
Cost of Equity	**10.69%**

Cost of Debt	
Cost of Debt (Interest Expense/Total Debt)	9.47%

Cost of Capital	
Cost of Equity	10.69%
Weight of Equity in Target Capital Structure	72.94%
Cost of Debt	9.47%
Weight of Debt in Capital Structure	27.06%
WACC	**10.36%**

WACC Calculation for CEAT Shares Valuation.

Step 6: Discounting the Cashflows

The WACC and the Cost of Equity for the company calculated in the above step are then used to discount the FCFF, FCFE and Terminal Value calculated in Step 3 and 4. In our case, we'll only consider the FCFF based Intrinsic price of the shares as it represents the cash flow to all the suppliers of capital and not only to the equity shareholders. Thus we arrive at Present value of future FCFF for CEAT Shares Valuation. (Units are INR Millions)

FCFF Calculation	FV	Discounted
Mar-20	4994.12	4525.37
Mar-21	1181.08	969.77
Mar-22	1643.38	1222.71
Mar-23	1796.76	1211.36
Mar-24	2030.79	1240.63
Terminal Value	39795.80	24311.66
Present Value (PV)		33481.50

FCFE Calculation	FV	Discounted
Mar-20	992.75	896.89
Mar-21	958.48	782.31
Mar-22	2082.07	1535.29
Mar-23	2138.61	1424.71
Mar-24	2363.92	1422.74
Terminal Value	39795.80	23951.31
Present Value (PV)		30013.25

PV of FCFF and FCFE for CEAT Shares Valuation.

Step 7: Arriving at the Intrinsic Value of the Shares

Dividing the PV of the FCFF and Terminal Value (the Value of the entire firm) by the number of outstanding shares we get the per share intrinsic value. We can compare this price with the current market price of the stock to get the Discount or Premium to its intrinsic price.

CEAT Shares Valuation	Units
PV in INR Million	33482
No of Shares Outstanding (In Million)	40

Intrinsic Value	837.04
Current Market Price of Share	1110.00
Current Discount/Premium	33%

Intrinsic Value of the Shares: CEAT Shares Valuation

CEAT Shares Valuation and Intrinsic Share Price = INR 837.04

AMBUJA CEMENT VALUATION

Ambuja Cement Valuation : About the Company

Ambuja Cements, formerly called as Gujarat Ambuja Cement,

is an Indian major cement manufacturer headquartered in Mumbai. The business model of the company is such that it mostly operates across 4 verticals namely product manufacturing, Support and Services, Ambuja Knowledge Initiative and Research & Innovation. The company manufactures Ambuja Cement which caters to caters to each of its three customer segments – Individual Home Builders (IHBs), Masons and Contractors, and Professionals. Other products include Ambuja Roof Special, Ambuja Cool Walls, BuildCem, PowerCem, Railcem and Alccofine micro materials.. From here, we go ahead with Ambuja Cement Valuation and Intrinsic Value of its shares.

Read more here: Ambuja Cement Shares Fundamental Analysis

Methodology Used:

Discounted cash flow (DCF) is a valuation method used to estimate the value of an investment based on its expected future cash flows. DCF analysis attempts to figure out the value of an investment today, based on projections of how much money it will generate in the future. The following step by step procedure is followed.

1. Determining the Revenue Growth Rates
2. Forecasting the Financial Statements
3. Deriving the FCFF and FCFE
4. Calculating the Terminal Value
5. Calculating the Discount Rate
6. Discounting the Cashflows
7. Arriving at the Intrinsic Value of the Shares

Step 1: Determining the Revenue Growth Rates

We arrive at the below table by using the past and expected future performance of both the company and the economy. This along with adjustments to changes in the management expectations, extraordinary events and other macro factors give the revenue growth rates for Ambuja Cement Valuation.

Financial Year	Revenue Growth Rate
Year 1	-4%
Year 2	16%
Year 3	14%
Year 4	13%
Year 5	13%

Revenue Growth Rates: Ambuja Cement Valuation

Step 2: Forecasting the Financial Statements

The financial statements are forecasted for a period of 5 years using the annual report data of the company. The assumptions used for forecasting are tabulated below. The Excel model is completely editable and can be adjusted for specific changes which may happen over a period of time.

Income Statement	
Average COGS as Percentage of Revenue	22.13%
Research and Development as Percentage of Revenue	0.00%
Sales, General and administrative as Percentage of Revenue	28.07%
Other operating expenses as Percentage of Revenue	38.67%
Other income (expense) as Percentage of Revenue	1.84%
Balance Sheet	
Short Term Debt as Percentage of Total Assets	3.25%
Long Term Debt as Percentage of Total Assets	0.07%
Cash and Cash Equivalents as Percentage of Revenue	31.20%
Short Term Equivalents as Percentage of Revenue	0.94%
Accounts Receivables as Percentage of Revenue	4.75%
Inventory as Percentage of Revenue	11.29%
Prepaid Expenses as Percentage of Revenue	4.36%
Other Current Assets as Percentage of Revenue	1.65%
Gross property, plant and equipment as Percentage of Revenue	78.13%
Intangible assets as Percentage of Revenue	8.33%
Other long-term assets as Percentage of Revenue	14.44%
Accounts payable as Percentage of Revenue	11.23%
Corporate Tax Rate	22.00%
Other current liabilities as Percentage of Revenue	17.49%
Retained Earnings as as Percentage of Net Income	81.47%
Accumulated other comprehensive income as Percentage of Revenue	29.44%
Cashflow Statement	
Other Working Capital as Percentage of Revenue	0.00%

Financial Statements Forecast : Ambuja Cement Valuation

Step 3: Deriving the FCFF and FCFE

Free cash flow to the firm (FCFF) represents the amount of cash flow from operations available for distribution after accounting for depreciation expenses, taxes, working capital, and investments. FCFF is a measurement of a company's profitability after all expenses and reinvestments. It is given as follows.

Free cash flow to equity (FCFE) is a measure of how much cash is available to the equity shareholders of a company after all expenses, reinvestment, and debt are paid. FCFE is a measure of equity capital usage.

F/S Items (INR Millions)	Mar-20	Mar-21	Mar-22	Mar-23	Mar-24
Free Cash Flow to Firm	31228	15605	26252	18312	20676
Free Cash Flow to Equity	38268	16332	26929	18958	21414

FCFF and FCFE values: Ambuja Cement Valuation

Step 4: Calculating the Terminal Value

Terminal value (TV) is the value of a business or project beyond the forecast period when future cash flows can be estimated. It assumes that a business will grow at a set growth rate forever after the forecast period. Terminal value often comprises a large percentage of the total assessed value.

Terminal Value Calculation	Units INR Millions
Free Cash Flow to Firm	20675.58
Growth Rate	5.00%
Cost of Capital	14.96%
Terminal Value	217916.75

Terminal Value: Ambuja Cement Valuation

Step 5: Calculating the Discount Rate

DCF analysis helps assess the viability of a project or investment by calculating the present value of expected future cash flows using a discount rate. Here we use the Weighted average cost of capital (WACC) to discount the cash flow. The below table from

the excel model shows the calculation of WACC for Ambuja Cement Valuation.

Cost of Equity Calcuation using CAPM	
Risk Free Rate (5 year G-Sec)	5.18%
Stock Beta (Ref: Reuters)	1.06
Beta Unlevered B/(1+ D(1-t)/E)	1.06
Beta Relevered B*(1+ D(1-t)/E)	1.31
Market Return Rm (Nifty 50 10 Year CAGR)	14.25%
Cost of Equity	**17.03%**

Cost of Debt	
Cost of Debt (Interest Expense/Total Debt)	**8.08%**

Cost of Capital	
Cost of Equity	17.03%
Weight of Equity in Target Capital Structure	76.90%
Cost of Debt	8.08%
Weight of Debt in Capital Structure	23.10%
WACC	**14.96%**

WACC Calculation for Ambuja Cement Valuation.

Step 6: Discounting the Cashflows

The WACC and the Cost of Equity for the company calculated in the above step are then used to discount the FCFF, FCFE and Terminal Value calculated in Step 3 and 4. In our case, we'll only consider the FCFF based Intrinsic price of the shares as it represents the cash flow to all the suppliers of capital and not only to the equity shareholders. Thus we arrive at Present value of future FCFF for Ambuja Cement Valuation. (Units are INR Millions)

FCFF Calculation	FV	Discounted
Mar-20	31227.68	27163.43
Mar-21	15604.81	11807.24
Mar-22	26251.89	17278.06
Mar-23	18311.85	10483.63
Mar-24	20675.58	10296.32
Terminal Value	217916.75	108521.25
Present Value (PV)		185549.92

FCFE Calculation	FV	Discounted
Mar-20	38268.06	32699.10
Mar-21	16331.93	11924.39
Mar-22	26928.53	16800.06
Mar-23	18958.40	10106.46
Mar-24	21413.89	9754.22
Terminal Value	217916.75	99263.01
Present Value (PV)		180547.24

PV of FCFF and FCFE for Ambuja Cement Valuation.

Step 7: Arriving at the Intrinsic Value of the Shares

Dividing the PV of the FCFF and Terminal Value (the Value of the entire firm) by the number of outstanding shares we get the per share intrinsic value. We can compare this price with the current market price of the stock to get the Discount or Premium to its intrinsic price.

Ambuja Cement Valuation	Units
PV in INR Million	185550
No of Shares Outstanding (In Million)	1986

Intrinsic Value	93.43
Current Market Price of Share	264.50
Current Discount/Premium	183%

Intrinsic Value of the Shares: Ambuja Cement Valuation

Ambuja Cement Valuation and Intrinsic Share Price = INR 93.43

EMAMI LTD VALUATION

Emami Ltd Valuation: About the Company

Emami was established in 1974 and is an Indian conglomerate company headquartered in Kolkata. It is one of the leading and fastest-growing personal and healthcare businesses in India, with a large portfolio of household brand names such as Boro-Plus, Navratna, Fair and Handsome, Zandu Balm, Mentho Plus

Balm, Fast Relief and Kesh King. The company, however, operates in a highly competitive environment of the FMCG sector in India against HUL, Dabur, Patanjali, Marico etc. From here, we go ahead with Emami Ltd Valuation and Intrinsic Value of its shares.

Read more here: Emami Ltd Shares Fundamental Analysis

Methodology Used:

Discounted cash flow (DCF) is a valuation method used to estimate the value of an investment based on its expected future cash flows. DCF analysis attempts to figure out the value of an investment today, based on projections of how much money it will generate in the future. The following step by step procedure is followed.

1. Determining the Revenue Growth Rates
2. Forecasting the Financial Statements
3. Deriving the FCFF and FCFE
4. Calculating the Terminal Value
5. Calculating the Discount Rate
6. Discounting the Cashflows
7. Arriving at the Intrinsic Value of the Shares

Step 1: Determining the Revenue Growth Rates

We arrive at the below table by using the past and expected future performance of both the company and the economy. This along with adjustments to changes in the management expectations, extraordinary events and other macro factors give the revenue growth rates for Emami Ltd Valuation.

Financial Year	Revenue Growth Rate
Year 1	-7%
Year 2	-6%
Year 3	13%
Year 4	12%
Year 5	12%

Revenue Growth Rates: Emami Ltd Valuation

Step 2: Forecasting the Financial Statements

The financial statements are forecasted for a period of 5 years using the annual report data of the company. The assumptions used for forecasting are tabulated below. The Excel model is completely editable and can be adjusted for specific changes which may happen over a period of time.

Assumptions Control Sheet	
Income Statement	
Average COGS as Percentage of Revenue	34.00%
Research and Development as Percentage of Revenue	0.00%
Sales, General and administrative as Percentage of Revenue	24.06%
Other operating expenses as Percentage of Revenue	24.00%
Other income (expense) as Percentage of Revenue	1.73%
Balance Sheet	
Short Term Debt as Percentage of Total Assets	8.05%
Long Term Debt as Percentage of Total Assets	5.99%
Cash and Cash Equivalents as Percentage of Revenue	5.15%
Short Term Equivalents as Percentage of Revenue	5.60%
Accounts Receivables as Percentage of Revenue	5.71%
Inventory as Percentage of Revenue	7.10%
Prepaid Expenses as Percentage of Revenue	2.21%
Other Current Assets as Percentage of Revenue	3.86%
Gross property, plant and equipment as Percentage of Revenue	32.76%
Intangible assets as Percentage of Revenue	37.98%
Other long-term assets as Percentage of Revenue	8.81%
Accounts payable as Percentage of Revenue	9.44%
Corporate Tax Rate	22.00%
Other current liabilities as Percentage of Revenue	8.44%
Retained Earnings as as Percentage of Net Income	25.69%
Accumulated other comprehensive income as Percentage of Revenue	41.31%
Cashflow Statement	
Other Working Capital as Percentage of Revenue	0.12%

Financial Statements Forecast : Emami Ltd Valuation

Step 3: Deriving the FCFF and FCFE

Free cash flow to the firm (FCFF) represents the amount of cash flow from operations available for distribution after accounting for depreciation expenses, taxes, working capital, and investments. FCFF is a measurement of a company's profitability after all expenses and reinvestments. It is given as follows.

Free cash flow to equity (FCFE) is a measure of how much cash is available to the equity shareholders of a company after all expenses, reinvestment, and debt are paid. FCFE is a measure of equity capital usage.

F/S Items (INR Millions)	Mar-20	Mar-21	Mar-22	Mar-23	Mar-24
Free Cash Flow to Firm	1314	2083	8221	5158	5775
Free Cash Flow to Equity	4350	1803	8477	4842	5657

FCFF and FCFE values: Emami Ltd Valuation

Step 4: Calculating the Terminal Value

Terminal value (TV) is the value of a business or project beyond the forecast period when future cash flows can be estimated. It assumes that a business will grow at a set growth rate forever after the forecast period. Terminal value often comprises a large percentage of the total assessed value.

Terminal Value Calculation	Units INR Millions
Free Cash Flow to Firm	5775.45
Growth Rate	5.00%
Cost of Capital	13.10%
Terminal Value	74857.59

Terminal Value: Emami Ltd Valuation

Step 5: Calculating the Discount Rate

DCF analysis helps assess the viability of a project or investment by calculating the present value of expected future cash flows using a discount rate. Here we use the Weighted average cost of capital (WACC) to discount the cash flow. The below table from

the excel model shows the calculation of WACC for Emami Ltd Valuation.

Cost of Equity Calcuation using CAPM	
Risk Free Rate (5 year G-Sec)	5.18%
Stock Beta (Ref: Reuters)	0.84
Beta Unlevered B/(1+ D(1-t)/E)	0.81
Beta Relevered B*(1+ D(1-t)/E)	0.94
Market Return Rm (Nifty 50 10 Year CAGR)	14.25%
Cost of Equity	**13.69%**

Cost of Debt	
Cost of Debt (Interest Expense/Total Debt)	10.28%

Cost of Capital	
Cost of Equity	13.69%
Weight of Equity in Target Capital Structure	82.68%
Cost of Debt	10.28%
Weight of Debt in Capital Structure	17.32%
WACC	**13.10%**

WACC Calculation for Emami Ltd Valuation.

Step 6: Discounting the Cashflows

The WACC and the Cost of Equity for the company calculated in the above step are then used to discount the FCFF, FCFE and Terminal Value calculated in Step 3 and 4. In our case, we'll only consider the FCFF based Intrinsic price of the shares as it represents the cash flow to all the suppliers of capital and not only to the equity shareholders. Thus we arrive at Present value of future FCFF for Emami Ltd Valuation. (Units are INR Millions)

FCFF Calculation	FV	Discounted
Mar-20	1313.71	1161.53
Mar-21	2082.97	1628.36
Mar-22	8220.66	5682.08
Mar-23	5157.66	3152.00
Mar-24	5775.45	3120.71
Terminal Value	74857.59	40448.60
Present Value (PV)		55193.28

FCFE Calculation	FV	Discounted
Mar-20	4349.74	3825.90
Mar-21	1803.37	1395.16
Mar-22	8476.88	5768.28
Mar-23	4841.59	2897.80
Mar-24	5656.98	2978.08
Terminal Value	74857.59	39408.22
Present Value (PV)		56273.44

PV of FCFF and FCFE for Emami Ltd Valuation.

Step 7: Arriving at the Intrinsic Value of the Shares

Dividing the PV of the FCFF and Terminal Value (the Value of the entire firm) by the number of outstanding shares we get the per share intrinsic value. We can compare this price with the current market price of the stock to get the Discount or Premium to its intrinsic price.

Emami Ltd Valuation	Units
PV in INR Million	55193
No of Shares Outstanding (In Million)	454

Intrinsic Value	121.57
Current Market Price of Share	163.00
Current Discount/Premium	34%

Intrinsic Value of the Shares: Emami Ltd Valuation

Emami Ltd Valuation and Intrinsic Share Price = INR 121.57

CIPLA VALUATION

Cipla Valuation : About the Company

Cipla is one of the largest pharmaceutical company in India. It has 46 states of the art manufacturing facilities across 5 countries and has 1500+ products. It employs 1300+ scientists and has seen double-digit growth in R&D investments in recent years. The major revenue share is about 38% from India, 21% from North America and 20% from Africa. It also has a presence in the European and other emerging markets in Asia. From here, we go ahead with Cipla Valuation and Intrinsic Value of its shares.

Read more here: **Cipla Shares Shares Fundamental Analysis**

Methodology Used:

Discounted cash flow (DCF) is a valuation method used to estimate the value of an investment based on its expected future cash flows. DCF analysis attempts to figure out the value of an investment today, based on projections of how much money it will generate in the future. The following step by step procedure is followed.

1. Determining the Revenue Growth Rates
2. Forecasting the Financial Statements
3. Deriving the FCFF and FCFE
4. Calculating the Terminal Value
5. Calculating the Discount Rate
6. Discounting the Cashflows
7. Arriving at the Intrinsic Value of the Shares

Step 1: Determining the Revenue Growth Rates

We arrive at the below table by using the past and expected future performance of both the company and the economy. This along with adjustments to changes in the management expectations, extraordinary events and other macro factors give the revenue growth rates for Cipla Valuation.

Financial Year	Revenue Growth Rate
Year 1	5%
Year 2	9%
Year 3	11%
Year 4	13%
Year 5	12%

Revenue Growth Rates: Cipla Valuation

Step 2: Forecasting the Financial Statements

The financial statements are forecasted for a period of 5 years using the annual report data of the company. The assumptions used for forecasting are tabulated below. The Excel model is completely editable and can be adjusted for specific changes which may happen over a period of time.

Assumptions Control Sheet	
Income Statement	
Average COGS as Percentage of Revenue	39.41%
Research and Development as Percentage of Revenue	1.75%
Sales, General and administrative as Percentage of Revenue	10.12%
Other operating expenses as Percentage of Revenue	36.07%
Other income (expense) as Percentage of Revenue	0.05%
Balance Sheet	
Short Term Debt as Percentage of Total Assets	7.47%
Long Term Debt as Percentage of Total Assets	11.15%
Cash and Cash Equivalents as Percentage of Revenue	4.78%
Short Term Equivalents as Percentage of Revenue	7.44%
Accounts Receivables as Percentage of Revenue	19.96%
Inventory as Percentage of Revenue	27.02%
Prepaid Expenses as Percentage of Revenue	1.18%
Other Current Assets as Percentage of Revenue	8.20%
Gross property, plant and equipment as Percentage of Revenue	46.21%
Intangible assets as Percentage of Revenue	16.78%
Other long-term assets as Percentage of Revenue	6.24%
Accounts payable as Percentage of Revenue	12.14%
Corporate Tax Rate	22.00%
Other current liabilities as Percentage of Revenue	8.47%
Retained Earnings as as Percentage of Net Income	81.99%
Accumulated other comprehensive income as Percentage of Revenue	22.50%
Cashflow Statement	
Other Working Capital as Percentage of Revenue	2.44%

Financial Statements Forecast :Cipla Valuation

Step 3: Deriving the FCFF and FCFE

Free cash flow to the firm (FCFF) represents the amount of cash flow from operations available for distribution after accounting for depreciation expenses, taxes, working capital, and investments. FCFF is a measurement of a company's profitability after all expenses and reinvestments. It is given as follows.

Free cash flow to equity (FCFE) is a measure of how much cash is available to the equity shareholders of a company after all expenses, reinvestment, and debt are paid. FCFE is a measure of equity capital usage.

F/S Items (INR Millions)	Mar-20	Mar-21	Mar-22	Mar-23	Mar-24
Free Cash Flow to Firm	28198	8290	11159	12695	13126
Free Cash Flow to Equity	31147	9618	12716	14927	15779

FCFF and FCFE values: Cipla Valuation

Step 4: Calculating the Terminal Value

Terminal value (TV) is the value of a business or project beyond the forecast period when future cash flows can be estimated. It assumes that a business will grow at a set growth rate forever after the forecast period. Terminal value often comprises a large percentage of the total assessed value.

Terminal Value Calculation	Units INR Millions
Free Cash Flow to Firm	13126.16
Growth Rate	6.00%
Cost of Capital	8.49%
Terminal Value	559322.37

Terminal Value: Cipla Valuation

Step 5: Calculating the Discount Rate

DCF analysis helps assess the viability of a project or investment by calculating the present value of expected future cash flows using a discount rate. Here we use the Weighted average cost of capital (WACC) to discount the cash flow. The below table from

the excel model shows the calculation of WACC for Cipla Valuation.

Cost of Equity Calcuation using CAPM	
Risk Free Rate (5 year G-Sec)	5.18%
Stock Beta (Ref: Reuters)	0.45
Beta Unlevered B/(1+ D(1-t)/E)	0.37
Beta Relevered B*(1+ D(1-t)/E)	0.45
Market Return Rm (Nifty 50 10 Year CAGR)	14.25%
Cost of Equity	**9.26%**

Cost of Debt	
Cost of Debt (Interest Expense/Total Debt)	5.80%

Cost of Capital	
Cost of Equity	9.26%
Weight of Equity in Target Capital Structure	77.63%
Cost of Debt	5.80%
Weight of Debt in Capital Structure	22.37%
WACC	**8.49%**

WACC Calculation for Cipla Valuation.

Step 6: Discounting the Cashflows

The WACC and the Cost of Equity for the company calculated in the above step are then used to discount the FCFF, FCFE and Terminal Value calculated in Step 3 and 4. In our case, we'll only consider the FCFF based Intrinsic price of the shares as it represents the cash flow to all the suppliers of capital and not only to the equity shareholders. Thus we arrive at Present value of future FCFF for Cipla Valuation. (Units are INR Millions)

FCFF Calculation	FV	Discounted
Mar-20	28197.63	25991.57
Mar-21	8290.07	7043.65
Mar-22	11158.98	8739.45
Mar-23	12695.31	9164.79
Mar-24	13126.16	8734.48
Terminal Value	559322.37	372187.33
Present Value (PV)		431861.28

FCFE Calculation	FV	Discounted
Mar-20	31147.39	28506.78
Mar-21	9617.69	8056.07
Mar-22	12715.54	9747.97
Mar-23	14927.15	10473.27
Mar-24	15778.95	10132.34
Terminal Value	559322.37	359165.04
Present Value (PV)		426081.48

PV of FCFF and FCFE for Cipla Valuation.

Step 7: Arriving at the Intrinsic Value of the Shares

Dividing the PV of the FCFF and Terminal Value (the Value of the entire firm) by the number of outstanding shares we get the per share intrinsic value. We can compare this price with the current market price of the stock to get the Discount or Premium to its intrinsic price.

Cipla Valuation	Units
PV in INR Million	431861
No of Shares Outstanding (In Million)	805

Intrinsic Value	536.47
Current Market Price of Share	793.00
Current Discount/Premium	48%

Intrinsic Value of the Shares: Cipla Valuation

Cipla Valuation and Intrinsic Share Price = INR 536.47

HAVELLS VALUATION

Havells Valuation: About the Company

Havells is a leading Fast Moving Electrical Goods (FMEG) Company and a major power distribution equipment manufacturer. The company enjoys significant market dominance across a wide spectrum of products, including Industrial and Domestic Circuit Protection Devices, Cables, Wires, Motors, Fans, Modular Switches, Home Appliances, Air Conditioners etc. The company owns some of the most well-known brands like Havells, Lloyd, Crabtree and Standard. From here, we go ahead with Havells Valuation and Intrinsic Value of its shares.

Read more here: **Havells Shares Fundamental Analysis**

Methodology Used:

Discounted cash flow (DCF) is a valuation method used to estimate the value of an investment based on its expected future cash flows. DCF analysis attempts to figure out the value of an investment today, based on projections of how much money it will generate in the future. The following step by step procedure is followed.

1. Determining the Revenue Growth Rates
2. Forecasting the Financial Statements
3. Deriving the FCFF and FCFE
4. Calculating the Terminal Value
5. Calculating the Discount Rate
6. Discounting the Cashflows
7. Arriving at the Intrinsic Value of the Shares

Step 1: Determining the Revenue Growth Rates

We arrive at the below table by using the past and expected future performance of both the company and the economy. This along with adjustments to changes in the management expect-

ations, extraordinary events and other macro factors give the revenue growth rates for Havells Valuation.

Financial Year	Revenue Growth Rate
Year 1	-5%
Year 2	10%
Year 3	16%
Year 4	14%
Year 5	14%

Revenue Growth Rates: Havells Valuation

Step 2: Forecasting the Financial Statements

The financial statements are forecasted for a period of 5 years using the annual report data of the company. The assumptions used for forecasting are tabulated below. The Excel model is completely editable and can be adjusted for specific changes which may happen over a period of time.

Assumptions Control Sheet	
Income Statement	
Average COGS as Percentage of Revenue	60.21%
Research and Development as Percentage of Revenue	0.00%
Sales, General and administrative as Percentage of Revenue	8.96%
Other operating expenses as Percentage of Revenue	20.68%
Other income (expense) as Percentage of Revenue	2.51%
Balance Sheet	
Short Term Debt as Percentage of Total Assets	2.17%
Long Term Debt as Percentage of Total Assets	1.53%
Cash and Cash Equivalents as Percentage of Revenue	5.30%
Short Term Equivalents as Percentage of Revenue	11.98%
Accounts Receivables as Percentage of Revenue	4.50%
Inventory as Percentage of Revenue	16.53%
Prepaid Expenses as Percentage of Revenue	0.68%
Other Current Assets as Percentage of Revenue	2.97%
Gross property, plant and equipment as Percentage of Revenue	22.69%
Intangible assets as Percentage of Revenue	6.05%
Other long-term assets as Percentage of Revenue	2.69%
Accounts payable as Percentage of Revenue	13.55%
Corporate Tax Rate	22.00%
Other current liabilities as Percentage of Revenue	9.08%
Retained Earnings as as Percentage of Net Income	59.82%
Accumulated other comprehensive income as Percentage of Revenue	15.19%
Cashflow Statement	
Other Working Capital as Percentage of Revenue	-2.92%

Financial Statements Forecast : Havells Valuation

Step 3: Deriving the FCFF and FCFE

Free cash flow to the firm (FCFF) represents the amount of cash flow from operations available for distribution after accounting for depreciation expenses, taxes, working capital, and investments. FCFF is a measurement of a company's profitability after all expenses and reinvestments. It is given as follows.

Free cash flow to equity (FCFE) is a measure of how much cash is available to the equity shareholders of a company after all expenses, reinvestment, and debt are paid. FCFE is a measure of equity capital usage.

F/S Items (INR Millions)	Mar-20	Mar-21	Mar-22	Mar-23	Mar-24
Free Cash Flow to Firm	8506	8370	9076	11070	13110
Free Cash Flow to Equity	10205	8427	9240	11243	13307

FCFF and FCFE values: Havells Valuation

Step 4: Calculating the Terminal Value

Terminal value (TV) is the value of a business or project beyond the forecast period when future cash flows can be estimated. It assumes that a business will grow at a set growth rate forever after the forecast period. Terminal value often comprises a large percentage of the total assessed value.

Terminal Value Calculation	Units INR Millions
Free Cash Flow to Firm	13109.72
Growth Rate	4.00%
Cost of Capital	15.5%
Terminal Value	118555.28

Terminal Value: Havells Valuation

Step 5: Calculating the Discount Rate

DCF analysis helps assess the viability of a project or investment by calculating the present value of expected future cash flows using a discount rate. Here we use the Weighted average cost of capital (WACC) to discount the cash flow. The below table

from the excel model shows the calculation of WACC for Havells Valuation.

Cost of Equity Calcuation using CAPM	
Risk Free Rate (5 year G-Sec)	5.18%
Stock Beta (Ref: Reuters)	1.14
Beta Unlevered B/(1+ D(1-t)/E)	1.12
Beta Relevered B*(1+ D(1-t)/E)	1.17
Market Return Rm (Nifty 50 10 Year CAGR)	14.25%
Cost of Equity	**15.81%**

Cost of Debt	
Cost of Debt (Interest Expense/Total Debt)	**10.24%**

Cost of Capital	
Cost of Equity	15.81%
Weight of Equity in Target Capital Structure	94.41%
Cost of Debt	10.24%
Weight of Debt in Capital Structure	5.59%
WACC	**15.50%**

WACC Calculation for Havells Valuation.

Step 6: Discounting the Cashflows

The WACC and the Cost of Equity for the company calculated in the above step are then used to discount the FCFF, FCFE and Terminal Value calculated in Step 3 and 4. In our case, we'll only consider the FCFF based Intrinsic price of the shares as it represents the cash flow to all the suppliers of capital and not only to the equity shareholders. Thus we arrive at Present value of future FCFF for Havells Valuation. (Units are INR Millions)

FCFF Calculation	FV	Discounted
Mar-20	8506.19	7364.65
Mar-21	8369.75	6274.03
Mar-22	9075.66	5890.20
Mar-23	11070.47	6220.64
Mar-24	13109.72	6377.93
Terminal Value	118555.28	57677.57
Present Value (PV)		**89805.02**

FCFE Calculation	FV	Discounted
Mar-20	10204.79	8811.53
Mar-21	8427.14	6283.12
Mar-22	9239.95	5948.56
Mar-23	11242.98	6249.87
Mar-24	13307.38	6387.48
Terminal Value	118555.28	56905.96
Present Value (PV)		**90586.52**

PV of FCFF and FCFE for Havells Valuation.

Step 7: Arriving at the Intrinsic Value of the Shares

Dividing the PV of the FCFF and Terminal Value (the Value of the entire firm) by the number of outstanding shares we get the per share intrinsic value. We can compare this price with the current market price of the stock to get the Discount or Premium to its intrinsic price.

Havells Valuation	Units
PV in INR Million	89805
No of Shares Outstanding (In Million)	625

Intrinsic Value	143.69
Current Market Price of Share	818.00
Current Discount/Premium	469%

Intrinsic Value of the Shares: Havells Valuation

Havells Valuation and Intrinsic Share Price = INR 143.69

ASHOK LEYLAND VALUATION

Ashok Leyland Valuation: About the Company

Ashok Leyland, the flagship of the Hinduja group, is the 2nd largest manufacturer of commercial vehicles in India and also the 3rd largest manufacturer of buses in the world. The company is also amongst the top 10 largest manufacturers of trucks globally. The company is headquartered in Chennai and has 9 manufacturing plants – 7 in India, a bus manufacturing facility in Ras Al Khaimah (UAE), one at Leeds, United Kingdom and a joint venture with the All teams Group. Ashok Leyland has a well-diversified portfolio across the automobile industry. The company has also been ranked as 34th best brand in India. From here, we go ahead with Ashok Leyland Valuation and Intrinsic Value of its shares.

Read more here: **Ashok Leyland Shares Fundamental Analysis**

Methodology Used:

Discounted cash flow (DCF) is a valuation method used to estimate the value of an investment based on its expected future cash flows. DCF analysis attempts to figure out the value of an investment today, based on projections of how much money it will generate in the future. The following step by step procedure is followed.

1. Determining the Revenue Growth Rates
2. Forecasting the Financial Statements
3. Deriving the FCFF and FCFE
4. Calculating the Terminal Value
5. Calculating the Discount Rate
6. Discounting the Cashflows
7. Arriving at the Intrinsic Value of the Shares

Step 1: Determining the Revenue Growth Rates

We arrive at the below table by using the past and expected future performance of both the company and the economy. This along with adjustments to changes in the management expectations, extraordinary events and other macro factors give the revenue growth rates for Ashok Leyland Valuation.

Financial Year	Revenue Growth Rate
Year 1	-40%
Year 2	15%
Year 3	16%
Year 4	13%
Year 5	13%

Revenue Growth Rates: Ashok Leyland Valuation

Step 2: Forecasting the Financial Statements

The financial statements are forecasted for a period of 5 years using the annual report data of the company. The assumptions used for forecasting are tabulated below. The Excel model is completely editable and can be adjusted for specific changes which may happen over a period of time.

Assumptions Control Sheet	
Income Statement	
Average COGS as Percentage of Revenue	70.81%
Research and Development as Percentage of Revenue	0.48%
Sales, General and administrative as Percentage of Revenue	6.73%
Other operating expenses as Percentage of Revenue	16.11%
Other income (expense) as Percentage of Revenue	6.40%
Balance Sheet	
Short Term Debt as Percentage of Total Assets	16.20%
Long Term Debt as Percentage of Total Assets	32.12%
Cash and Cash Equivalents as Percentage of Revenue	5.74%
Short Term Equivalents as Percentage of Revenue	5.10%
Accounts Receivables as Percentage of Revenue	7.03%
Inventory as Percentage of Revenue	10.22%
Prepaid Expenses as Percentage of Revenue	2.59%
Other Current Assets as Percentage of Revenue	20.36%
Gross property, plant and equipment as Percentage of Revenue	26.43%
Intangible assets as Percentage of Revenue	2.58%
Other long-term assets as Percentage of Revenue	42.75%
Accounts payable as Percentage of Revenue	17.02%
Corporate Tax Rate	22.00%
Other current liabilities as Percentage of Revenue	10.43%
Retained Earnings as as Percentage of Net Income	56.52%
Accumulated other comprehensive income as Percentage of Revenue	6.08%
Cashflow Statement	
Other Working Capital as Percentage of Revenue	11.68%

Financial Statements Forecast : Ashok Leyland Valuation

Step 3: Deriving the FCFF and FCFE

Free cash flow to the firm (FCFF) represents the amount of cash flow from operations available for distribution after accounting for depreciation expenses, taxes, working capital, and investments. FCFF is a measurement of a company's profitability after all expenses and reinvestments. It is given as follows.

Free cash flow to equity (FCFE) is a measure of how much cash is available to the equity shareholders of a company after all expenses, reinvestment, and debt are paid. FCFE is a measure of equity capital usage.

F/S Items (INR Millions)	Mar-20	Mar-21	Mar-22	Mar-23	Mar-24
Free Cash Flow to Firm	-33473	19519	22388	24712	26295
Free Cash Flow to Equity	-86749	18386	33906	21493	27284

FCFF and FCFE values: Ashok Leyland Valuation

Step 4: Calculating the Terminal Value

Terminal value (TV) is the value of a business or project beyond the forecast period when future cash flows can be estimated. It assumes that a business will grow at a set growth rate forever after the forecast period. Terminal value often comprises a large percentage of the total assessed value.

Terminal Value Calculation	Units INR Millions
Free Cash Flow to Firm	26294.62
Growth Rate	5.00%
Cost of Capital	11.82%
Terminal Value	404814.63

Terminal Value: Ashok Leyland Valuation

Step 5: Calculating the Discount Rate

DCF analysis helps assess the viability of a project or investment by calculating the present value of expected future cash flows using a discount rate. Here we use the Weighted average cost of capital (WACC) to discount the cash flow. The below table from

the excel model shows the calculation of WACC for Ashok Leyland Valuation.

Cost of Equity Calcuation using CAPM	
Risk Free Rate (5 year G-Sec)	6.00%
Stock Beta (Ref: Reuters)	1.41
Beta Unlevered B/(1+ D(1-t)/E)	0.52
Beta Relevered B*(1+ D(1-t)/E)	1.24
Market Return Rm (Nifty 50 10 Year CAGR)	14.25%
Cost of Equity	**16.25%**

Cost of Debt	
Cost of Debt (Interest Expense/Total Debt)	9.33%

Cost of Capital	
Cost of Equity	16.25%
Weight of Equity in Target Capital Structure	35.97%
Cost of Debt	9.33%
Weight of Debt in Capital Structure	64.03%
WACC	**11.82%**

WACC Calculation for Ashok Leyland Valuation.

Step 6: Discounting the Cashflows

The WACC and the Cost of Equity for the company calculated in the above step are then used to discount the FCFF, FCFE and Terminal Value calculated in Step 3 and 4. In our case, we'll only consider the FCFF based Intrinsic price of the shares as it represents the cash flow to all the suppliers of capital and not only to the equity shareholders. Thus we arrive at Present value of future FCFF for Ashok Leyland Valuation. (Units are INR Millions)

FCFF Calculation	FV	Discounted
Mar-20	-33473.33	-29934.94
Mar-21	19519.15	15610.62
Mar-22	22387.95	16012.27
Mar-23	24712.35	15806.38
Mar-24	26294.62	15040.58
Terminal Value	404814.63	231554.92
Present Value (PV)		264089.82

FCFE Calculation	FV	Discounted
Mar-20	-86748.84	-74620.27
Mar-21	18385.87	13604.12
Mar-22	33906.20	21580.35
Mar-23	21493.20	11767.22
Mar-24	27283.84	12849.06
Terminal Value	404814.63	190643.52
Present Value (PV)		175824.00

PV of FCFF and FCFE for Ashok Leyland Valuation.

Step 7: Arriving at the Intrinsic Value of the Shares

Dividing the PV of the FCFF and Terminal Value (the Value of the entire firm) by the number of outstanding shares we get the per share intrinsic value. We can compare this price with the current market price of the stock to get the Discount or Premium to its intrinsic price.

Ashok Leyland Valuation	Units
PV in INR Million	264090
No of Shares Outstanding (In Million)	2935

Intrinsic Value	89.98
Current Market Price of Share	84.15
Current Discount/Premium	-6%

Intrinsic Value of the Shares: Ashok Leyland Valuation

Ashok Leyland Valuation and Intrinsic Share Price = INR 89.98

BAJAJ AUTO VALUATION

Bajaj Auto Valuation: About the Company

Bajaj Auto has 3 large manufacturing facilities in India with a total capacity of 6.4+ million motorcycles per annum. The Waluj plant manufactures commercial vehicles like 3- wheelers, passenger carriers and good carriers and has a capacity of 9.3 lakh units a year. Bajaj is a market leader in its commercial vehicle segment with a market share of 58% in India. The company also has a dedicated R&D unit which focuses on efficiency improvements and new models. The new launches, CT 110, Platina 110 H and Pulsar 125 have been received well in the domestic market. From here, we go ahead with Bajaj Auto Valuation and Intrinsic Value of its shares.

Read more here: **Bajaj Auto Shares Fundamental Analysis**

Methodology Used:

Discounted cash flow (DCF) is a valuation method used to estimate the value of an investment based on its expected future cash flows. DCF analysis attempts to figure out the value of an investment today, based on projections of how much money it will generate in the future. The following step by step procedure is followed.

1. Determining the Revenue Growth Rates
2. Forecasting the Financial Statements
3. Deriving the FCFF and FCFE
4. Calculating the Terminal Value
5. Calculating the Discount Rate
6. Discounting the Cashflows
7. Arriving at the Intrinsic Value of the Shares

Step 1: Determining the Revenue Growth Rates

We arrive at the below table by using the past and expected future performance of both the company and the economy. This along with adjustments to changes in the management expect-

ations, extraordinary events and other macro factors give the revenue growth rates for Bajaj Auto Valuation.

Financial Year	Revenue Growth Rate
Year 1	-13%
Year 2	22%
Year 3	13%
Year 4	12%
Year 5	13%

Revenue Growth Rates: Bajaj Auto Valuation

Step 2: Forecasting the Financial Statements

The financial statements are forecasted for a period of 5 years using the annual report data of the company. The assumptions used for forecasting are tabulated below. The Excel model is completely editable and can be adjusted for specific changes which may happen over a period of time.

Assumptions Control Sheet	
Income Statement	
Average COGS as Percentage of Revenue	71.03%
Research and Development as Percentage of Revenue	2.50%
Sales, General and administrative as Percentage of Revenue	2.46%
Other operating expenses as Percentage of Revenue	6.97%
Other income (expense) as Percentage of Revenue	4.05%
Balance Sheet	
Short Term Debt as Percentage of Total Assets	0.00%
Long Term Debt as Percentage of Total Assets	0.00%
Cash and Cash Equivalents as Percentage of Revenue	2.82%
Short Term Equivalents as Percentage of Revenue	17.54%
Accounts Receivables as Percentage of Revenue	5.38%
Inventory as Percentage of Revenue	3.31%
Prepaid Expenses as Percentage of Revenue	0.36%
Other Current Assets as Percentage of Revenue	4.48%
Gross property, plant and equipment as Percentage of Revenue	18.04%
Intangible assets as Percentage of Revenue	0.37%
Other long-term assets as Percentage of Revenue	49.17%
Accounts payable as Percentage of Revenue	10.90%
Corporate Tax Rate	22.00%
Other current liabilities as Percentage of Revenue	3.50%
Retained Earnings as as Percentage of Net Income	43.23%
Accumulated other comprehensive income as Percentage of Revenue	21.26%
Cashflow Statement	
Other Working Capital as Percentage of Revenue	-0.76%

Financial Statements Forecast :Bajaj Auto Valuation

Step 3: Deriving the FCFF and FCFE

Free cash flow to the firm (FCFF) represents the amount of cash flow from operations available for distribution after accounting for depreciation expenses, taxes, working capital, and investments. FCFF is a measurement of a company's profitability after all expenses and reinvestments. It is given as follows.

Free cash flow to equity (FCFE) is a measure of how much cash is available to the equity shareholders of a company after all expenses, reinvestment, and debt are paid. FCFE is a measure of equity capital usage.

F/S Items (INR Millions)	Mar-20	Mar-21	Mar-22	Mar-23	Mar-24
Free Cash Flow to Firm	-45237	61550	73325	65416	76834
Free Cash Flow to Equity	-45237	61550	73325	65416	76834

FCFF and FCFE values: Bajaj Auto Valuation

Step 4: Calculating the Terminal Value

Terminal value (TV) is the value of a business or project beyond the forecast period when future cash flows can be estimated. It assumes that a business will grow at a set growth rate forever after the forecast period. Terminal value often comprises a large percentage of the total assessed value.

Terminal Value Calculation	Units INR Millions
Free Cash Flow to Firm	76833.83
Growth Rate	5.50%
Cost of Capital	14.07%
Terminal Value	946008.53

Terminal Value: Bajaj Auto Valuation

Step 5: Calculating the Discount Rate

DCF analysis helps assess the viability of a project or investment by calculating the present value of expected future cash flows using a discount rate. Here we use the Weighted average cost of capital (WACC) to discount the cash flow. The below table from

the excel model shows the calculation of WACC for Bajaj Auto Shares Valuation.

Cost of Equity Calcuation using CAPM	
Risk Free Rate (5 year G-Sec)	5.18%
Stock Beta (Ref: Reuters)	0.98
Beta Unlevered B/(1+ D(1-t)/E)	0.98
Beta Relevered B*(1+ D(1-t)/E)	0.98
Market Return Rm (Nifty 50 10 Year CAGR)	14.25%
Cost of Equity	**14.07%**

Cost of Debt	
Cost of Debt (Interest Expense/Total Debt)	0.00%

Cost of Capital	
Cost of Equity	14.07%
Weight of Equity in Target Capital Structure	100.00%
Cost of Debt	0.00%
Weight of Debt in Capital Structure	0.00%
WACC	**14.07%**

WACC Calculation for Bajaj Auto Valuation.

Step 6: Discounting the Cashflows

The WACC and the Cost of Equity for the company calculated in the above step are then used to discount the FCFF, FCFE and Terminal Value calculated in Step 3 and 4. In our case, we'll only consider the FCFF based Intrinsic price of the shares as it represents the cash flow to all the suppliers of capital and not only to the equity shareholders. Thus we arrive at Present value of future FCFF for Bajaj Auto Valuation. (Units are INR Millions)

FCFF Calculation	FV	Discounted
Mar-20	-45236.80	-39657.54
Mar-21	61550.47	47304.14
Mar-22	73325.17	49403.16
Mar-23	65415.69	38638.26
Mar-24	76833.83	39785.23
Terminal Value	946008.53	489851.56
Present Value (PV)		625324.81

FCFE Calculation	FV	Discounted
Mar-20	-45236.80	-39657.54
Mar-21	61550.47	47304.14
Mar-22	73325.17	49403.16
Mar-23	65415.69	38638.26
Mar-24	76833.83	39785.23
Terminal Value	946008.53	489851.56
Present Value (PV)		625324.81

PV of FCFF and FCFE for Bajaj Auto Valuation.

Step 7: Arriving at the Intrinsic Value of the Shares

Dividing the PV of the FCFF and Terminal Value (the Value of the entire firm) by the number of outstanding shares we get the per share intrinsic value. We can compare this price with the current market price of the stock to get the Discount or Premium to its intrinsic price.

Bajaj Auto Valuation	Units
PV in INR Million	625325
No of Shares Outstanding (In Million)	289

Intrinsic Value	2163.75
Current Market Price of Share	2930.00
Current Discount/Premium	35%

Intrinsic Value of the Shares: Bajaj Auto Valuation

Bajaj Auto Valuation and Intrinsic Share Price = INR 2163.75

AUROBINDO PHARMA VALUATION

Aurobindo Pharma Valuation: About the Company

The company operates in the pharmaceutical business where market dominance is achieved through R&D, regulatory approvals, scale and distribution. Aurobindo Pharma is the 7th largest generic company by sales in the world and the 2nd largest Indian Pharmaceutical company in terms of revenue. It is also the 2nd largest generic Company by Rx dispensed in the US. This shows the sheer scale of operations which the company has along with a wide distribution across the globe. From here, we go ahead with Aurobindo Pharma Valuation and Intrinsic Value of its shares.

Read more here: **Aurobindo Pharma Shares Fundamental Analysis**

Methodology Used:

Discounted cash flow (DCF) is a valuation method used to estimate the value of an investment based on its expected future cash flows. DCF analysis attempts to figure out the value of an investment today, based on projections of how much money it will generate in the future. The following step by step procedure is followed.

1. Determining the Revenue Growth Rates
2. Forecasting the Financial Statements
3. Deriving the FCFF and FCFE
4. Calculating the Terminal Value
5. Calculating the Discount Rate
6. Discounting the Cashflows
7. Arriving at the Intrinsic Value of the Shares

Step 1: Determining the Revenue Growth Rates

We arrive at the below table by using the past and expected future performance of both the company and the economy. This along with adjustments to changes in the management expectations, extraordinary events and other macro factors give the revenue growth rates for Aurobindo Pharma Valuation.

Financial Year	Revenue Growth Rate
Year 1	10%
Year 2	14%
Year 3	15%
Year 4	14%
Year 5	15%

Revenue Growth Rates: Aurobindo Pharma Valuation

Step 2: Forecasting the Financial Statements

The financial statements are forecasted for a period of 5 years using the annual report data of the company. The assumptions used for forecasting are tabulated below. The Excel model is completely editable and can be adjusted for specific changes which may happen over a period of time.

Assumptions Control Sheet	
Income Statement	
Average COGS as Percentage of Revenue	46.80%
Research and Development as Percentage of Revenue	0.21%
Sales, General and administrative as Percentage of Revenue	5.48%
Other operating expenses as Percentage of Revenue	27.85%
Other income (expense) as Percentage of Revenue	-0.20%
Balance Sheet	
Short Term Debt as Percentage of Total Assets	23.40%
Long Term Debt as Percentage of Total Assets	3.02%
Cash and Cash Equivalents as Percentage of Revenue	6.58%
Short Term Equivalents as Percentage of Revenue	0.03%
Accounts Receivables as Percentage of Revenue	23.00%
Inventory as Percentage of Revenue	33.15%
Prepaid Expenses as Percentage of Revenue	0.02%
Other Current Assets as Percentage of Revenue	10.45%
Gross property, plant and equipment as Percentage of Revenue	39.49%
Intangible assets as Percentage of Revenue	6.25%
Other long-term assets as Percentage of Revenue	3.54%
Accounts payable as Percentage of Revenue	15.46%
Corporate Tax Rate	22.00%
Other current liabilities as Percentage of Revenue	9.84%
Retained Earnings as as Percentage of Net Income	93.22%
Accumulated other comprehensive income as Percentage of Revenue	5.82%
Cashflow Statement	
Other Working Capital as Percentage of Revenue	0.46%

Financial Statements Forecast : Aurobindo Pharma Valuation

Step 3: Deriving the FCFF and FCFE

Free cash flow to the firm (FCFF) represents the amount of cash flow from operations available for distribution after accounting for depreciation expenses, taxes, working capital, and investments. FCFF is a measurement of a company's profitability after all expenses and reinvestments. It is given as follows.

Free cash flow to equity (FCFE) is a measure of how much cash is available to the equity shareholders of a company after all expenses, reinvestment, and debt are paid. FCFE is a measure of equity capital usage.

F/S Items (INR Millions)	Mar-20	Mar-21	Mar-22	Mar-23	Mar-24
Free Cash Flow to Firm	-10726	7837	15675	14031	16457
Free Cash Flow to Equity	-2720	15863	42755	18874	27106

FCFF and FCFE values: Aurobindo Pharma Valuation

Step 4: Calculating the Terminal Value

Terminal value (TV) is the value of a business or project beyond the forecast period when future cash flows can be estimated. It assumes that a business will grow at a set growth rate forever after the forecast period. Terminal value often comprises a large percentage of the total assessed value.

Terminal Value Calculation	Units INR Millions
Free Cash Flow to Firm	16457.19
Growth Rate	5.00%
Cost of Capital	11.35%
Terminal Value	271943.49

Terminal Value: Aurobindo Pharma Valuation

Step 5: Calculating the Discount Rate

DCF analysis helps assess the viability of a project or investment by calculating the present value of expected future cash flows using a discount rate. Here we use the Weighted average cost of capital (WACC) to discount the cash flow. The below table from

the excel model shows the calculation of WACC for Aurobindo Pharma Valuation.

Cost of Equity Calcuation using CAPM	
Risk Free Rate (5 year G-Sec)	6.00%
Stock Beta (Ref: Reuters)	0.84
Beta Unlevered B/(1+ D(1-t)/E)	0.61
Beta Relevered B*(1+ D(1-t)/E)	0.83
Market Return Rm (Nifty 50 10 Year CAGR)	14.25%
Cost of Equity	**12.82%**

Cost of Debt	
Cost of Debt (Interest Expense/Total Debt)	8.23%

Cost of Capital	
Cost of Equity	12.82%
Weight of Equity in Target Capital Structure	68.13%
Cost of Debt	8.23%
Weight of Debt in Capital Structure	31.87%
WACC	**11.35%**

WACC Calculation for Aurobindo Pharma Valuation.

Step 6: Discounting the Cashflows

The WACC and the Cost of Equity for the company calculated in the above step are then used to discount the FCFF, FCFE and Terminal Value calculated in Step 3 and 4. In our case, we'll only consider the FCFF based Intrinsic price of the shares as it represents the cash flow to all the suppliers of capital and not only to the equity shareholders. Thus we arrive at Present value of future FCFF for Aurobindo Pharma Valuation. (Units are INR Millions)

FCFF Calculation	FV	Discounted
Mar-20	-10725.89	-9632.22
Mar-21	7837.30	6320.52
Mar-22	15674.51	11352.02
Mar-23	14031.17	9125.70
Mar-24	16457.19	9612.16
Terminal Value	271943.49	158834.24
Present Value (PV)		185612.42

FCFE Calculation	FV	Discounted
Mar-20	-2719.87	-2410.89
Mar-21	15863.18	12463.69
Mar-22	42754.72	29776.13
Mar-23	18873.59	11651.10
Mar-24	27106.48	14832.47
Terminal Value	271943.49	148805.51
Present Value (PV)		215118.01

PV of FCFF and FCFE for Aurobindo Pharma Valuation.

Step 7: Arriving at the Intrinsic Value of the Shares

Dividing the PV of the FCFF and Terminal Value (the Value of the entire firm) by the number of outstanding shares we get the per share intrinsic value. We can compare this price with the current market price of the stock to get the Discount or Premium to its intrinsic price.

Aurobindo Pharma Valuation	Units
PV in INR Million	185612
No of Shares Outstanding (In Million)	586

Intrinsic Value	316.74
Current Market Price of Share	782.00
Current Discount/Premium	147%

Intrinsic Value of the Shares: Aurobindo Pharma Valuation

Aurobindo Pharma Valuation and Intrinsic Share Price = INR 316.74

COAL INDIA VALUATION

COAL India Valuation

Coal India Valuation: About the Company

Coal India Limited (CIL) is the state-owned coal mining company promoted by the Indian Government. With a modest production of 79 Million Tonnes (MTs) in the year of its incorporation, Coal India has today grown to become the largest coal producer in the world. CIL is a Maharatna company – a privileged status conferred by the Government of India to select state-owned enterprises in order to empower them to expand their operations and emerge as global giants. From here, we go ahead with Coal India Valuation and Intrinsic Value of its shares.

Read more here: **Coal India Shares Fundamental Analysis**

Methodology Used:

Discounted cash flow (DCF) is a valuation method used to estimate the value of an investment based on its expected future cash flows. DCF analysis attempts to figure out the value of an investment today, based on projections of how much money it will generate in the future. The following step by step procedure is followed.

1. Determining the Revenue Growth Rates
2. Forecasting the Financial Statements
3. Deriving the FCFF and FCFE
4. Calculating the Terminal Value
5. Calculating the Discount Rate
6. Discounting the Cashflows
7. Arriving at the Intrinsic Value of the Shares

Step 1: Determining the Revenue Growth Rates

We arrive at the below table by using the past and expected future performance of both the company and the economy. This along with adjustments to changes in the management expectations, extraordinary events and other macro factors give the revenue growth rates for Coal India Valuation.

Financial Year	Revenue Growth Rate
Year 1	-8%
Year 2	13%
Year 3	15%
Year 4	15%
Year 5	14%

Revenue Growth Rates: Coal India Valuation

Step 2: Forecasting the Financial Statements

The financial statements are forecasted for a period of 5 years using the annual report data of the company. The assumptions used for forecasting are tabulated below. The Excel model is completely editable and can be adjusted for specific changes which may happen over a period of time.

Assumptions Control Sheet	
Income Statement	
Average COGS as Percentage of Revenue	15.49%
Research and Development as Percentage of Revenue	0.05%
Sales, General and administrative as Percentage of Revenue	0.23%
Other operating expenses as Percentage of Revenue	67.43%
Other income (expense) as Percentage of Revenue	6.57%
Balance Sheet	
Short Term Debt as Percentage of Total Assets	0.81%
Long Term Debt as Percentage of Total Assets	0.55%
Cash and Cash Equivalents as Percentage of Revenue	4.46%
Short Term Equivalents as Percentage of Revenue	39.65%
Accounts Receivables as Percentage of Revenue	10.65%
Inventory as Percentage of Revenue	8.37%
Prepaid Expenses as Percentage of Revenue	5.08%
Other Current Assets as Percentage of Revenue	17.39%
Gross property, plant and equipment as Percentage of Revenue	46.12%
Intangible assets as Percentage of Revenue	0.04%
Other long-term assets as Percentage of Revenue	16.26%
Accounts payable as Percentage of Revenue	5.76%
Corporate Tax Rate	22.00%
Other current liabilities as Percentage of Revenue	38.80%
Retained Earnings as as Percentage of Net Income	38.04%
Accumulated other comprehensive income as Percentage of Revenue	24.31%
Cashflow Statement	
Other Working Capital as Percentage of Revenue	-3.50%

Financial Statements Forecast : Coal India Valuation

Step 3: Deriving the FCFF and FCFE

Free cash flow to the firm (FCFF) represents the amount of cash flow from operations available for distribution after accounting for depreciation expenses, taxes, working capital, and investments. FCFF is a measurement of a company's profitability after all expenses and reinvestments. It is given as follows.

Free cash flow to equity (FCFE) is a measure of how much cash is available to the equity shareholders of a company after all expenses, reinvestment, and debt are paid. FCFE is a measure of equity capital usage.

F/S Items (INR Millions)	Mar-20	Mar-21	Mar-22	Mar-23	Mar-24

Free Cash Flow to Firm	-344	76609	105845	130287	241163
Free Cash Flow to Equity	-3885	77586	107074	131713	241564

FCFF and FCFE values: Coal India Valuation

Step 4: Calculating the Terminal Value

Terminal value (TV) is the value of a business or project beyond the forecast period when future cash flows can be estimated. It assumes that a business will grow at a set growth rate forever after the forecast period. Terminal value often comprises a large percentage of the total assessed value.

Terminal Value Calculation	Units INR Millions
Free Cash Flow to Firm	241162.63
Growth Rate	4.00%
Cost of Capital	13.16%
Terminal Value	2736727.98

Terminal Value: Coal India Valuation

Step 5: Calculating the Discount Rate

DCF analysis helps assess the viability of a project or investment by calculating the present value of expected future cash flows using a discount rate. Here we use the Weighted average cost of capital (WACC) to discount the cash flow. The below table from the excel model shows the calculation of WACC for Coal India Valuation.

Cost of Equity Calcuation using CAPM	
Risk Free Rate (5 year G-Sec)	5.18%
Stock Beta (Ref: Reuters)	0.93
Beta Unlevered B/(1+ D(1-t)/E)	0.87
Beta Relevered B*(1+ D(1-t)/E)	0.90
Market Return Rm (Nifty 50 10 Year CAGR)	14.25%
Cost of Equity	**13.38%**

Cost of Debt	
Cost of Debt (Interest Expense/Total Debt)	8.41%

Cost of Capital	
Cost of Equity	13.38%
Weight of Equity in Target Capital Structure	95.61%
Cost of Debt	8.41%
Weight of Debt in Capital Structure	4.39%
WACC	**13.16%**

WACC Calculation for Coal India Valuation.

Step 6: Discounting the Cashflows

The WACC and the Cost of Equity for the company calculated in the above step are then used to discount the FCFF, FCFE and Terminal Value calculated in Step 3 and 4. In our case, we'll only consider the FCFF based Intrinsic price of the shares as it represents the cash flow to all the suppliers of capital and not only to the equity shareholders. Thus we arrive at Present value of future FCFF for Coal India Valuation. (Units are INR Millions)

FCFF Calculation	FV	Discounted
Mar-20	-343.57	-303.60
Mar-21	76608.59	59821.40
Mar-22	105844.85	73036.24
Mar-23	130286.78	79443.53
Mar-24	241162.63	129944.46
Terminal Value	2736727.98	1474617.55
Present Value (PV)		1816559.58

FCFE Calculation	FV	Discounted
Mar-20	-3885.46	-3426.85
Mar-21	77586.28	60351.93
Mar-22	107074.23	73458.87
Mar-23	131713.03	79696.84
Mar-24	241563.87	128913.21
Terminal Value	2736727.98	1460484.97
Present Value (PV)		1799478.97

PV of FCFF and FCFE for Coal India Valuation.

Step 7: Arriving at the Intrinsic Value of the Shares

Dividing the PV of the FCFF and Terminal Value (the Value of the entire firm) by the number of outstanding shares we get the per share intrinsic value. We can compare this price with the current market price of the stock to get the Discount or Premium to its intrinsic price.

Coal India Valuation	Units
PV in INR Million	1816560
No of Shares Outstanding (In Million)	6206

Intrinsic Value	292.71
Current Market Price of Share	121.00
Current Discount/Premium	-59%

Intrinsic Value of the Shares: Coal India Valuation

Coal India Valuation and Intrinsic Share Price = INR 292.71

End of Book 1

www.ingramcontent.com/pod-product-compliance
Lightning Source LLC
Chambersburg PA
CBHW072029230526
45466CB00020B/1160